"[Feinberg] succeeds in keeping the reader engaged, entertained, and edified . . . [She] raises questions that linger in the mind after the book is closed."

PUBLISHERS WEEKLY

Margaret Feinberg is a modern-day David. With eyes on the heavens, His Word in hand, and all her heart turned towards His, she tells the wonders of His love in ways you've never known. Who in the world doesn't need joy like this?

ANN VOSKAMP
Author of *One Thousand Gifts*

"Feinberg turns exegesis into an art, delivering findings that invite the audience to touch, taste, smell, and see God's handiwork throughout the Scriptures and in their own lives."

ED STETZER
President, LifeWay Research

We dangerously underestimate the power of wonder . . . Margaret recenters wonder at the heart of our relationship with God, with seismic results. This book shook my soul awake and made it impossible for me to continue following a God of my own design. Her work is captivating, staggeringly honest and refreshingly deep, stirring my mind, heart, sense, and soul to consider God in ways that are reshaping me.

NANCY ORTBERG
Author of *Looking for God*

Wonderstruck invites you to open your eyes to the delights, joys, and gifts of God all around. You can't read this book and remain the same—it will change you so you see yourself, others, God, and the world around you in a more beautiful, life-giving way.

BOB GOFF
Author of *Love Does*

Wonderstruck is a game-changing book. Feinberg's brilliant writing captures you as she points to the God who has captured her.

JUD WILHITE
Senior pastor of Central Christian Church, Las Vegas, Nevada

This generation longs to encounter Good News in fresh, modern, and engaging ways. Margaret Feinberg stands at the forefront of communicating the timeless truths of Jesus with vibrant language, imagery, and expression. Those who read *Wonderstruck* will never be the same. Highly recommended.

GABE LYONS
Founder of Q; author of *The Next Christians*

Wonderstruck, like all of Margaret's writing, is rooted in historical, global, and biblical perspectives, and reads like a song with storied verses and a beautiful chorus: Pay attention, pay attention; it matters; pay attention. I can't wait to share this book with friends.

SARA GROVES
Singer and songwriter

Margaret Feinberg does a superb job of helping us hear God. Through her felicitous prose and engaging storytelling, I not only got a feeling for her unique journey with God, but I also received fresh glimpses into my own.

MARK GALLI
Senior managing editor, *Christianity Today*

Maybe the reason the Christian faith in America is so anemic and lifeless is because we have settled for lifeless religion and stuffy ritual instead of a thriving, close, alive, passionate relationship to the living God. Margaret's latest book is like standing under Niagara Falls spiritually. You won't be able to put it down.

RAY JOHNSTON
Senior pastor of Bayside Church

WONDERSTRUCK

WONDERSTRUCK

AWAKEN TO THE NEARNESS
of GOD

MARGARET
FEINBERG

WORTHY
PUBLISHING

Published by Worthy Publishing, a division of Worthy Media, Inc., 134 Franklin Road, Suite 200, Brentwood, Tennessee 37027.

HELPING PEOPLE EXPERIENCE THE HEART OF GOD

eBook available at www.worthypublishing.com

Audio distributed through Oasis Audio; visit www.oasisaudio.com

---

Library of Congress Control Number: 2012950268

Some names and details in anecdotes shared in this volume have been changed to protect identities.

For foreign and subsidiary rights, contact Riggins International Rights Service, Inc., www.rigginsrights.com

ISBN: 978-1-61795-088-9 (trade paper)

Published in association with ChristopherFerebee.com, Attorney and Literary Agent

Cover Design: Mary Hooper/Milkglass Creative
Cover Image: iStock Photo
Interior Typesetting: Susan Browne Design

Printed in the United States of America

12 13 14 15 16 SBI 8 7 6 5 4 3 2 1

CONTENTS

BONUS TRACKS

WONDERSTRUCK

.000:
CAPTURED BY THE
NIGHT SKY

BRIGHT-EYED IN THE EARLY HOURS of a frigid January morning several years ago, I heard a familiar voice whisper, "It's time to go to sleep." Though I knew such words were spoken in wisdom and love, I refused to allow the allure of slumberland to steal me from the wonder.

The announcement of a promotion for my husband, Leif, had required a move, and we had spent every waking hour boxing up all we owned and saying good-bye to loved ones. We weren't moving far: ninety-two miles to be exact. But in southeast Alaska, where the only way to travel between islands is by air, boat, or long frigid swim, miles multiply in people's hearts.

Rumors circled of the inefficiency and unreliability of the ferry system connecting the regional ports, but remained the only practical option for the move. Pulling our overloaded vehicles into the belly of the ship, we had exhaled a sigh of relief and then scrambled to the observatory deck to secure a window seat where we could watch the last of the brief day's blissful sun melt into the horizon.

The route we had selected wasn't the most direct but permitted us to leave Sitka one day and wake up in our new hometown of Juneau the next. Staring out the window, I couldn't remember the last time I'd slouched in a chair with nowhere to go and nothing to do. The ship held me captive, and I submitted to the monotony. Then fatigue drained the remaining amps of my energy reserves. I took one last glance at Leif and mustered a slanted smile before nodding off to sleep.

Hunger soon woke me. Following the dim lighting down the passageway, I navigated through rows of sleeping strangers and their bags to make my way to the commissary. After a quick bite to eat, I returned to my seat. Before nestling in, I admired the faint moonlight backlighting the mountainous coast. Then something compelled me to look up, and a scene unfolded that I suspect caused at least one angel to gasp: the expanse of the sky transformed from inky blackness into an infinite canvas on which brushstrokes of apricot, sapphire, and emerald painted themselves into the night sky. Like an oil painting in progress, the colors refused to stand still. The hues danced as if listening to jazz. Iridescent shades sharpened then faded with wild fervor.

This wasn't the first time I had been mesmerized by the northern lights. When traveling to Alaska years before, the promise of such celestial beauty had ignited my imagination. I met Leif (pronounced *lay-f*) on one of my first visits to the great state. Before our friendship turned romantic, we'd sit at the end of the road in Sitka—away from the town's lights—hoping for a glimpse of the midnight delights. One evening I noticed a brushstroke of lime green in the sky growing brighter with each passing moment. I rubbed my eyes as if I'd seen a mirage then looked again. The color appeared to flap in the wind like a loose sail.

"That's the northern lights," Leif assured me.

The beauty of the aurora borealis enchanted me. Since that evening, I had spent countless hours peering through the window of our home and returning to the desolate place where the road ends to catch one more glimpse of the beauty that quickened my soul. Even on the most extravagant evenings, the northern lights had lasted only an hour or two then faded, but on this evening the curtain to the performance never closed. The sky exhaled more hues than I imagined possible, and I found myself caught up in the wonder.[1]

That's when I heard Leif whisper, "It's time to go to sleep."

"Look!" I protested.

Leif craned his neck, staring into the starry night. Arms locked, we squished against the window to watch nature's fireworks.

"It's two thirty in the morning," Leif whispered. "We should sleep."

"Go ahead. I'll nod off soon."

Leif knew me all too well: I had no intention of ever closing my eyes. Aware of the privilege of watching God's creation unfold its glorious mysteries, I didn't want to miss a millisecond. Wonderstruck by my Creator, this moment of spiritual awakening stirred in me a longing to experience more of God. If these lights were so beautiful, how much more stunning must their Maker be? What kind of God paints the sky in such effulgent hues? For some, the northern lights are a tourist attraction, but for me, they are a portal to the very heart of God. My lips remained motionless, but my soul sang as I witnessed this revival in the night sky.

The hours passed. I offered up a silent prayer to lay hold of the wonder of God, to find myself once again awed by another facet of his nature, another glimpse of his presence in our world.

Even though I lived in Alaska for five years and witnessed the northern lights more than a hundred times, none compared to that night. I still savor the encounter and live in hopeful anticipation of another. Though we now live at a lower latitude on the outskirts of a major city notorious for its light pollution, on many nights, you'll still find me scouting the sky in hope of catching another glimpse of the wonder.

It occurred to me that this is the posture we're supposed to take in our spiritual journeys. God delights for us to cup our hands in prayer and scrunch our faces against the vault of heaven in holy expectation that he will meet us in beautiful, mysterious ways. The Creator desires to captivate us not just with his handiwork but with himself—displaying facets of his character, igniting us with his fiery love, awakening us to the intensity of his holiness.

Often such incidents occur when we least anticipate, leaving us wonderstruck much like my encounter with the northern lights. But the insistent invitation of the Spirit is to stay alert! Eyes wide open. Hands pressed against the glass. We never know when or how God, like the aurora borealis, will appear. But we can live each day trusting that the God who met us in the past will once again greet us with arms wide open in the future.[2]

God extends endless invitations to encounter him, yet too often we sleep straight through. Unconscious of the life God wants for us, we slumber in the presence of the sacred and snore in the company of the divine. We remain asleep while God roosts in our midst. Inactive and inert, we become spiritual sleepyheads who clamor for the snooze button rather than climb out of bed. In our dormant states, we miss the opportunities to experience his many gifts and to know the Giver more fully.

The wonder of God is that moment of spiritual awakening that makes us curious to know God more.

Alaska doesn't have a monopoly on such moments, and neither does the night sky. They are all around us—not just in the sanctuary and sacraments. God stoops beside our beds as we offer our evening prayers; he nestles on the couch as we open our homes to strangers, neighbors, friends; he waits in our laughter and tears, our thank yous and I love yous.

What are the wonders of God in your own life that you fail to marvel or even sleep straight through? How often do you pass by God's presence and handiwork unaware?

Despite the breathtaking moments of God that I've experienced, all too often I find myself like so many of the other passengers on the ferry, deep in sleep, missing the moment. I succumb to exhaustion rather than remain alert to the wondrous displays that reveal more of God. In those moments, the burning bushes in my life are reduced to smoldering distractions, and the still, small voice becomes something I absentmindedly shush.

I recently began noticing this in my life in increasing measure. I no longer waited on God with hopeful expectation. Icy religion replaced the delightful warmth of being a child of God. Though I expressed gratitude at the appropriate moments, in the depths of my spirit, I wasn't appreciative. Words of praise may have lingered on my lips during worship, but when the song ended, so did any trace of enthusiasm.

The sense of holy awe was replaced by unholy indifference. Hope diminished to a manageable emotion. Love became a fleeting expression in short supply.

Yet God met me there.

God's infinite nature knows neither beginning nor end; our Creator is like a vast ocean, fathomless and without bounds, an ever-rising tide without abatement, yet in my spiritual journey in the months after our move, I stood ankle deep, baptized only in the shallows of his presence. I sensed the Spirit beckoning me to plunge into the cool, shadowy depths marked by indescribable beauty, those unforgettable moments of life that draw us closer to God. Allured by the Spirit, I lunged forward.

And I prayed for wonder.

Sometimes the simplest petitions prove to be the most critical. If I had known what I was asking or how God would answer, I don't know if I would have had the courage to make the request.

I have a hunch that I'm not the only one who has misplaced the marvel of a life lived with God. Faith invites us into an enchanting journey—one marked by mysteries of divine beauty, holy courage, irrepressible hope, unending love. But in my life, any sense of the splendor of God had faded. I knew I needed a fresh encounter with God to awaken me from my sleep, to disturb me from my slumber.

And so I prayed for wonder.

Palms extended, wide-eyed with expectation, I waited for an answer. And God did not disappoint. For me, a prayer for wonder asks the Lord to expand my capacity to see and savor the divine gifts all around. I still relish the striking and curious ways God answered. The means God employed to alert me to the beauty awaiting in the most mundane moments of life. The process God used to transform my hollowness to hallowedness.

Through the months and years that followed, Bible passages that had become stale and flat came alive much like a pop-up book revealing hidden beauty and unexpected surprises.

Often when God answers a prayer for wonder, the tone and tenacity with which we live our lives changes. Holiness beckons. Divine expectation flourishes. Hope returns. Love abounds. In response, we awaken, toss back the covers, climb out of bed, and drink in the fullness of life God intended for us. We live alert to the wonders all around us and within us that expand our desire to know God more.

My hope is that through the following pages you will rediscover, or possibly discover for the first time, the wonder of God stirring in your own heart. Apart from this wonder, passion for God and his Word fades. But with a renewed sense of wonder, even the cold embers of an extinguished faith can be fanned back into flame.

Will you pray for wonder? Right now, ask God to awaken your ability to see and savor his sweet presence and recognize his divine handiwork.

And as you pray, may you be wonderstruck. With each page, may you discover another facet of God's character, feel the soft pinch of his presence, and step back in astonishment of the One who holds everything together. Along the way, I trust you'll experience God.

When you lay hold of him, may you never let go.

Blessings,
Margaret

.001:
HIDDEN AMONG
THE HIGHLANDS

The Wonder of Divine Expectation

INVIGORATED BY THE COOL, damp morning air and kind-hearted conversation, I followed the stony path up the side of the mountain, calculating the placement of each step. Looking up, I realized I had been transported somewhere otherworldly.

What began as a few pine trees transformed into an enchanted forest. Uneven from uncounted layers of fallen leaves, twigs, and trees, the ground was pacified by a thick tapestry of emerald and malachite mosses and grasses. Toadstools and wild mushrooms crouched in the shadows. Lichens defied gravity as they clung to the undersides of tree branches and then trailed onto the ground, providing woodsy wall-to-wall carpeting that created the thick silence.

Turning to my new acquaintance, Juliet, I suggested that if we weren't careful perhaps a mischievous gnome might pop out of the woods and steal our trail mix when we weren't looking.

She laughed before joining in the imaginative fun. By the time we passed the next kilometer marker, we had created an entire world of hobbits, elves, and mysterious creatures that moved so fast they were invisible to the naked eye. In our fanciful world, Tolkien-inspired hobbits battled elves over the ancient border of Bogle Glen, which boasted the sweetest, tallest grass in all the land and a hollow tree that led to a mysterious lower cavern. The evil creature Ewich, named after a sign we passed on the trail, developed an appetite for grilled elf and enlisted the help of the bridge trolls to capture hobbits. The only way the elves and hobbits could survive was by signing a truce and battling Ewich and the trolls together.

Without the steady ascent of the trail, which forced me to focus my limited energies on breathing and finding steady footholds on slippery rock, I would have dreamed about this imaginary world for hours, developing an entire universe of characters and conflicts, battles and beautiful moments.

The otherworldliness of the forest was only one of the many wonders that lined our eighty-kilometer journey of the Highland Way, a historic region of Scotland that boasts thick woods, rolling hills, sparse moorlands, and countless lochs, or lakes, spreading through the countryside.

Nearly a year before, Summit Leaders founder Joel Malm had contacted me about hosting a spiritual leadership expedition. The unique nonprofit provides people with an opportunity to step out of their normal routines and gain a fresh perspective on life. Rather than attend a conference where they become part of the crowd, those who came on the expedition would have a different experience. We would host a smaller group, enjoy face-to-face conversation, and share the pains and joys of a long hike.

On our initial phone call, Joel supplied behind-the-scenes details of his recent adventure on the Inca Trail ascending Machu Picchu. The trip included rafting, paragliding, and camping. As the sun dipped below the horizon, the group gathered around the fire for a time of spiritual reflection.

While intrigued by the opportunity, I couldn't keep the reticence out of my voice as we chatted.

"What would your dream expedition look like?" he asked.

Having grown up in Colorado, I was well versed in sleeping in tents and river bathing, but my dream expedition would be, well, more posh. Each day's hike would be challenging but not to the point of exhaustion. We'd carry daypacks chock-full of water, sandwiches, and a blend of sweet-and-salty snacks. Someone else would take care of our luggage. At night we'd skip sleeping bags and nestle into a cozy bed and breakfast. The majority of meals would come from a menu, and most important, we'd enjoy lots of chocolate and other treats.

"Still there?"

"Yeah," he said, drinking in all I had shared. "I'm not sure about the treats or chocolate, but I think the place you want to go is the Highlands of Scotland."

I didn't know much about the Scottish Highlands and had never dreamed of leading a spiritual pilgrimage overseas, but as Joel described the expedition along the historic route, my imagination sparkled at the possibility. Further details poured in over the following weeks. I found myself saying yes to Joel without any tangible idea of what I was saying yes to.

And then we were there, standing in the Edinburgh airport introducing ourselves to one another—seven women along with two men who served as our support team. Our task: hike eighty kilometers (fifty miles) of the Highland Way, which ended in Fort William at the foot of Great Britain's tallest mountain, Ben Nevis.

The drive to our first night's lodging, located near the trail-head, hinted at the diverse beauty we'd encounter. Stout forests. Quiet glens. Austere rock summits. Sapphire lakes too numerous to count. The inn where we stayed that night brought comfort to our hungry stomachs and travel-weary bodies. When Joel handed me the key to my room, I had no idea what to expect but was delighted to discover a small room, immaculate, with a single twin-sized bed and private bathroom.

I rested my luggage on the grey floor and tried to factor in the time change as I calculated how long until dinner. Forty-five minutes. Just enough time to prepare for the evening devotion that followed the meal. One last time I prayerfully considered what to share and reflected on the work God had been doing in my life.

Several years earlier I had been in a place in my spiritual journey where God seemed nonexistent. I was still carving out time to connect with God each day. Reading Scripture. Praying. Solitude. Though I emptied my bag of spiritual discipline tricks, nothing seemed to change. I arrived at church empty and left unsatisfied. I read from Psalms. Proverbs. Obadiah. The Gospels. Even Leviticus. Nothing connected. Worship was meh. Conversations felt flat.

Where do I go, God? What do I do? All I heard was crushing silence, the kind that's empty and full, quiet and deafening all at the same time.

Weeks rolled into months. Though discouraged, I refused to stop pursuing God. One morning, the thought struck me: maybe it's time to go back to the beginning.

Plodding through the first fifty chapters of the Bible, I began catching glimpses of the wonders of God I had never seen before—mysteries of creation, promises of redemption, the depths of God's love for humankind. Like the first drops of blue ink spilled into a carafe of water, the beauty infused my mind and heart.

Finishing Genesis, I felt compelled to return to the beginning. I read and reread, weaving in commentaries from the likes of Walter Brueggemann, Bruce Waltke, and Nahum Sarna. The more I explored Genesis, the more I felt I was on a morning hike, looking around to see a moss-carpeted forest, wholly present and fully captivated by the mystery and marvel of it all.

That morning became an eighteen-month-long, personal in-depth look at the book of the Bible whose name is drawn from the first word of Scripture, in Hebrew, *beresheet*, meaning "in the beginning." Genesis, I discovered, is more than the story of our origins, where we began, the formation of our cosmos and humanity. The first book is also the story of various barriers that we keep running into, in our relationship with God, each other, and creation, as well as God's loving decision to tear down those walls, redeem a mad world, and draw us closer to himself.

Strewn across the white comforter on the Scottish hotel bed, I breezed through the first few chapters of Genesis and sensed the sacred echo "It is good" with regard to my plan of sharing from these passages over the upcoming week.

Realizing I was a few minutes late for dinner, I rushed down to the restaurant where the group gathered around a series of small tables pushed up against each other. We were the only ones in the hotel's dining hall, and when a perky young waitress appeared, she greeted us with unintelligible words that sounded like an encrypted form of English. One of the team members, Katie, interpreted: the chef was running late.

Throughout the evening I only understood every third word the waitress spoke and resorted to nodding and smiling through the other two. I managed to navigate the menu with help from the team. The less adventurous among us, *ahem*, skipped the Scottish standards of haggis and blood sausage for more familiar fare like salad, steak, salmon, and a selection of potatoes cooked a hundred different ways.

Our bellies full, we searched for the quietest room we could find. One of the team members urged us into a vacant card room attached to the hotel lobby. Because the room held only a single brown leather couch and two red leather chairs, we pulled in extra seating from the lobby so we could gather around a narrow glass table.

After explaining my personal journey through Genesis, we took turns reading portions of the first chapter of the Bible. Then we discussed the theological facets the words reveal about our God—a God in whom all things are made and held together, a God who creates goodness and celebrates it at every turn, a God of profound order who triumphs over chaos, a God of boundless generosity and unfathomable power. As we examined the passage, I sensed the familiar scripture awaken something deep inside me.

I asked everyone to share personal hopes, dreams, and desires for the trip as a springboard for a time of prayer. I listened intently. In secret I hoped someone would give words to the thoughts somersaulting through my mind, but no one did.

Then my turn came. "My hope . . . my prayer," I stammered.

I felt the iron weight of the pause as I grasped for the perfect way to express what I desired from God. I took a deep breath and plunged.

"This sounds strange," I apologized, "but I'm praying for pixie dust."

I might as well have vacuumed all the air out of the room. While a few stared uncomfortably at me, more than a dozen eyes darted back and forth in an almost unanimous expression: *what have we gotten ourselves into?*

I kept talking. "More than anything, what I long for is our God, the One who bedazzled the heavens and razzle-dazzled the earth, to meet us in such a way during our time in Scotland that we find ourselves awestruck by his goodness and generosity, his provision and presence. I'm praying for pixie dust. I want to leave here with a sense of wonderment as we encounter and experience things only God can do."

One by one the members of the team exhaled, a welcome sign they were extending grace to me. A few even smiled.

Louie, a pastor whose short grey hair and mustache framed twinkling youthful eyes, broke the silence. "Margaret, I think what you're asking for is something me and my boys pray for often. You're asking for the favor of God. We pray for God's favor both in good times and bad—that we'd sense the reality that we're one of God's children, one of God's favorites, and wait expectantly for what God will do."

With those words, Louie became one of my favorite members of the team. In closing our devotional time together, we prayed with boldness for pixie dust.

When I returned to my room that night, I tucked myself into bed. The European down comforter left me feeling warm, snug, and enveloped by a thousand feathers. God had reawakened a sense of divine expectation. Though God had been at work in my life in countless ways—revealing so many wonders—I realized that deep down inside I still backed away from living each day with holy anticipation.

Praying for pixie dust was an invitation for God to lavish our team with his loving-kindness, and for each of us to walk more upright, eyes attentive to what God might do next. You can't pray for pixie dust and maintain a dour demeanor or dreary disposition. The Mary Poppins of all prayers, asking for pixie dust is hard to do without a frolicsome smile on your face, a playful cheer in your spirit, a holy anticipation of how God may answer.

Now, praying for pixie dust is not magic whereby if you say the right words—"abracadabra," "suoicodilaipxecitsiligarfilacrepus,"[1] or "a la peanut butter sandwiches"[2]—something marvelous happens. That's wishful thinking. A prayer marked by faith is never about what happens on our terms or time lines, but God's. Faith-stained prayer brings us to a place of trust and hope. Praying for pixie dust is a childlike expression of trust and hope—trusting in both God's wisdom and winsomeness, finding hope in God's mercy and mirth.

I often think of Jesus surrounded by eager dads and moms, men and women the disciples dismiss as pushy parents. The Gospel of Mark, an account of the life of Jesus known for its brevity, pauses to highlight the important details of the scene.[3]

Surrounded by an informal congregation, Jesus teaches on the mystery of marriage, reminding listeners of their holy commitment, not just before humans but before God. The crowd responds en masse, but it's easy to miss. Moms and dads elbow their way to the front of the crowd, hoping Jesus will rest his hands on their children and pray for them. The parents respond to Jesus by placing the fruit of their marriages, their most valuable possessions, and their entire futures, in the hands of the Son of God.

The disciples don't recognize the preciousness of the parents' response and issue a sharp-tongued reprimand. Jesus is peeved. The Son of God calls the people to repentance, and they respond but not in the way the disciples anticipate. Jesus defends the children, and their parents too, when he tells the disciples to leave the children alone and let them come to him.

The Gospel of Mark records Jesus picking up kids. I imagine Jesus whispering the love of God in their ears. As he prays, some of the children probably tug on his beard; others poke at his cheeks. A few remain skeptical of the stranger and keep their eyes on Mommy at all times. Jesus gives the kids huge bear hugs and twirls the most rambunctious in the air before returning them to their parents. At least, that's how I imagine this scene when I read, "And He took them in His arms and began blessing them, laying His hands on them."[4]

Against a backdrop of hugs and laughter, Jesus makes a startling declaration: The kingdom of God belongs to those who maintain childlike receptivity. Those who refuse to receive the kingdom of God like a child will miss it entirely.

I don't think the disciples intentionally discriminated against the little ones; they may have meant well in trying to protect Jesus from being overrun. After all, if Jesus swung one child in his arms, all the kids would want a turn.

Standing in stark contrast to the eagerness and exuberance of the children is the disciples' curt response. Modern management buzzwords can be used to describe their reasoning. They're leveraging Jesus' time, streamlining the day's activities, creating a win-win for the rabbi and the multitude, maintaining the ministry's best practices. But Jesus knows something far more valuable is at stake than spiritual productivity or return on investment.

With their heads down, eyes straining for the next step, the disciples lost sight of the wonderment that Jesus came for all of humanity: the bourgeoisie and the peasant, the grumpy and the ebullient, the grey-haired and the bedheads. Despite the miles and meals they shared, those closest to Jesus had lost their childlike receptivity, their ability to recognize that both God's response to us and our response to God is seldom what we anticipate.

The story stands as a potent reminder of the importance of humility and trust, as well as a personal wake-up call that all too often I'm far more like the disciples than the children. I fail to enter into God's kingdom. Distracted by efficiency and effectiveness, I lose out on what the children enjoyed that day— simply being with Jesus, delighting in his presence, and humbly asking him to pray for me.

Maybe the best place to rediscover the kingdom of God is bouncing on Jesus' knee.

For me, praying for pixie dust was an expression of childlike receptivity. More than anything, I wanted Jesus to catch me up in his arms and twirl me in the air.

The next morning, like a bottle rid of the cork, we began our hike bubbling with energy and overflowing with enthusiasm. After the first kilometer or two, each of us settled into a steady pace, discovering our individual cadence on the trail. We also discovered we weren't alone. The Scottish masterminds behind the Highland Way were not concerned with drawing clear lines between public and private property. We grew accustomed to walking through strangers' backyards. I even caught a pair of seven-year-old blue eyes peeking from behind a fence post. We managed to sneak in a wave and grin before the figure disappeared in the shadows.

The more entrepreneurial locals along the trail had turned their backyards into trading posts. Add a few makeshift bath- rooms to a piece of property, and you've got a hiking destination, or what I prefer to call a "running destination" because I ran for all of them along the trail.

The first trading post we visited was an add-on building to the back of a brown wooden barn. A weathered picnic table embellished with fresh rain droplets provided a limited seating area. After using the "glory hallelujah," my new name for any- thing that resembled indoor plumbing, I scoured the limited inventory shelf-by-shelf for the perfect comfort food.

Next to the door rested a plywood storage shelf with a dozen cubbies. Each cubby displayed a basket of produce ranging from potatoes to cabbage, dark lettuce leaves to green beans. I grabbed a translucent orange carrot on a whim and circled back to the counter to pay the bored teenage salesclerk.

Brushing off a few grains of dirt, I bit through the carrot's skin to discover a mouthful of confectionery nutty crunchiness. Returning to the basket, I purchased the remaining stock and shared them with the team. None of us could remember when a common carrot had tasted so good. With each bite, we savored the sweetness of God's creation.

Midafternoon we passed by the moss-covered ruins of an abbey and an ancient cemetery. Soon after, our feet began to ache with the kind of soreness that whispers the next step will hurt even more. Our pace slowed, and other travelers began to pass us. One of the team members struck up a conversation with a pair of sixty-somethings whose worn boots and tan lines suggested they'd been on the trail much longer. To raise awareness for an incurable disease, they were hiking from the tip of England to the tip of Scotland. They passed us on day fifty-three of their three-month journey and left us effortlessly in their dust. Invigorated, we forgot about our feet.

The sun flirted with us throughout the day, glancing from behind clouds like a child playing peekaboo. For more than two hours, the golden orb, which seldom makes an appearance in the United Kingdom, graced us with its presence. One of the ladies, Peggy, responded to the royal treatment by lying down on a soft patch of grass on the side of the road. I brushed the annoyance at the delay far, far away and took the spot next to her. One by one we lay next to Peggy, eyes closed, bodies melting into the land. I don't know how long we were there, embraced by the holy moment of rest, but my cheeks felt warm and my head tingly when we returned to our feet. We stepped back on the trail with a divine awareness we didn't have before—the discovery that when journeying with God some of the best parts of any pilgrimage are the detours.

Our fearless leader, Joel, had arrived in Scotland with a cough and bronchial ache that intensified with each passing day. I became overly conscious of what for him were unconscious actions: coughing, sniffling, rubbing his nose. Joel conceded to seeing a doctor but not until medical help was hard to find.

After persistent phone calls, he located a Scottish doctor who agreed to see him on short notice. Joel sat patiently in the waiting room before being ushered into a small office with dated equipment.

The doctor wore a typical white coat, stethoscope hanging like a horseshoe around his neck. For more than an hour after his quick exam, the doctor peppered Joel with questions that had nothing to do with his medical condition. The doctor wanted to know about the expedition, the team members, the peculiarities of the Highland Way. When Joel was dismissed, the doctor shoved a bottle of antibiotics into his hand then told the receptionist to charge Joel one pound for the visit, the equivalent of about $1.65 at the time. God's provision surprised us all. The next day Joel began feeling better. I couldn't help but think the medicine and the bill were coated in pixie dust.

Our longest and most difficult hike of the journey was a thirty-eight-kilometer stretch between the Bridge of Orchy and Glen Coe. The day began with patchy skies and a few light showers that were soon replaced with ominous clouds and pouring rain. We found shelter in the King's House, one of Scotland's oldest licensed inns, which had some much-needed glory hallelujahs. The manager showed us favor by allowing us to bring in some of our own food to enjoy alongside the pub fare. Our quick stop became a two-hour Scottish smorgasbord of delicacies ranging from fresh-grilled venison burgers to the salt-and-vinegar chips we packed with us.

When we returned to the trail, we met the greatest challenge of the hike, Devil's Staircase, a steep, rocky climb compounded by rivulets, gusty wind, and pelting hail. Yet the treacherous miles and icy conditions were made easier by conversation, encouragement, and singing tunes that ranged from hymns to Queen.

At every turn we experienced all the ingredients of divine pixie dust: grace and kindness, generosity and favor. In the evenings we returned to Genesis, exploring the faithfulness and goodness of God.

By the time we returned to Edinburgh to fly home, I felt an inward glow. The days had been long. The mileage challenging. But something about the adventure cultivated life, not just a flicker or flash, but a beaming hope of life with a future. The wonder of divine expectation took up residence inside me.

On our final night together, Joel's plans to dine at a specific Italian restaurant were thwarted by our tight schedule. We found ourselves searching the streets of Edinburgh for a restaurant. The most enthusiastic foodies ran ahead from one outdoor menu display to the next, narrowing down the selection.

Juliet found a French restaurant tucked away on a quiet cobblestone street. We gathered cozily around a wooden table. The white linens gossiped of the tasty food to come. After placing our orders, we sat around like people who had known each other for years. We told stories and cracked jokes. Our voices bounced off the stone floor, joining the chorus of what had become a full restaurant.

"Look!" Joel said. His eyes were wide as he pointed toward pieces of framed art across the room. "Do you know what that says?"

We turned to what grabbed his attention. Above a row of photography featuring faces from around the world sat four larger pieces of framed art. Each featured French words scrawled in colored pencil, finger paint, and crayon, perhaps by children, on backgrounds of black, white, yellow, and blue. I squinted to read but, seeing it was French, stopped and looked to Joel for a translation.

Joel leaned forward to interpret the paintings:

"In the beginning, God created the heavens and the earth. Now the earth was formless and void . . ." He continued reading until our bodies were covered with goose pimples. The final painting read, "On the seventh day, God rested."

We flew across the Atlantic, drove 605 miles, and hiked 50 more to arrive in a French restaurant in Scotland that greeted us with the seven days of creation in Genesis—the very passages we explored that week. As if that weren't enough, the name of the restaurant was *Le Sept,* "The Seven."

I felt as though we were living a fairy tale.

The server delivered the finest food any of us had eaten in a long time, and we celebrated. We deliciated in the lavish love of God. Our bellies satisfied, we exited the restaurant and searched for the nearest bus stop.

We stood next to the road, craning our necks for Bus 42.

Behind us stood a large library with giant oaken doors.

Next thing we knew, Joel was pointing again, this time toward large letters on the front of the building:

"Let there be light."

We were wonderstruck. Our jaws dropped. Each word seemed to call us by name.

As if carving himself into the side of a building right before our eyes, God revealed himself again. Now he didn't appear out of nowhere. Rather, in this holy exclamation point of a moment, God came into focus in such a way that we could not deny he'd been with us the whole time.

God had been hiding in plain sight along the Highland Way. None of our encounters was chance; none of our experiences accidental. God not only heard the petition for pixie dust but answered in ways that stirred the wonder of divine expectation in all of our hearts.

The experience revealed I still lived with a lid on my prayer life. Petitioning for pixie dust removes any sense of "praying it safe." Asking God to unleash his mercy and grace and goodness and love is like boldly looking into the eyes of God and saying, "Surprise me!" The wonder is that he does, if we have eyes to see. Whether in the shining eyes of a baby, a sunset that stops our conversation, or an eight-day trek culminating in holy goose bumps, God reveals his grandeur. And these revelations beckon us to go deeper with him.

Many of us say we want to experience God, but we don't

look for his majesty. We travel life's paths with our heads down, focused on the next step with our careers or families or retirement plans. But we don't *really* expect God to show up with divine wonder.

God invites us to look up, open our eyes to the wonder all around us, and seize every opportunity to encounter him. This isn't a passive expectation but an active one, the kind prompting us to elbow our way to Jesus, knowing he longs to meet us with a hearty embrace and sometimes even twirl us through the air.

How many of us are praying for pixie dust? How many of us expect Jesus to show up and display his presence and power? How many of us are living alert to God and his work in every area of our lives?

The wonder of divine expectation isn't in the way we ask but in the way God answers. While in Scotland, we didn't just pray for pixie dust, we lived fully awake for God's response. When we encountered those divine moments, we didn't dismiss them as coincidence but gave thanks for even the subtlest expressions of God's loving care.

We expected Jesus to show up—and he did! From organic carrots to one-pound medical bills to French artwork, God interacted with us, blessed us, and swung us in his arms. I believe this is the kind of life we're meant for—not just on the Highland Way but every day.

God is not merely at your fingertips but within your grasp. Live each day like a child digging through a treasure chest, rifling for the next discovery. Open your arms and your eyes to the God who stands in plain sight and works miracles in your midst. Look for him in your workdays and weekends, in your meeting-filled Mondays and your lazy Saturdays. Search for him in the snowy sunsets and Sabbaths, seasons of Lent and sitting at your table. Pray for—and expect—wonder. For when you search for God, you *will* discover him.

Live awake and aware because the wonder awaits.

.002:
SHOCK AND AWE

The Wonder of God's Presence

MY FOREARMS AND KNEES pressed hard against the oak floor. The wave of emotion I desperately tried to shove back crashed over me. My body convulsed involuntarily. I rolled onto my back, laboring for breath. The grief overcame me: I gave in to the weeping.

Time becomes immeasurable for those who mourn. To this day I have no idea how long I lay there, ceiling blurring in and out of focus, until my body went limp. Wholly spent, my mind wandered through the events that had brought me there. This wasn't my first encounter with affliction, loss, or pain, but what made the experience overwhelming was the level of shock and awe. Overloaded by relentless adversity, I fell prey to what the military describes as a spectacular display of force that paralyzes an adversary's perception of the battlefield, destroying its will to fight.

The series of circumstances that reduced me to a salty pool of tears had begun months before with a collection of life's

smaller inconveniences. A few months earlier, Leif was returning from a weekend of volunteering when the transmission in
our car failed. Stranded nearly two hours from our home, the
vehicle required towing back to Denver. Two weeks later we
were still waiting for our car, our *only* car, to return from the
repair shop. Though this was barely an inconvenience compared
to the events yet to come, in the back of my mind I couldn't help
but ask *why*. Why does life crumble sometimes?

A day before we picked up the vehicle, I ventured downstairs to place fresh linens on our guest bed and experienced an
unfamiliar sensation: my socks felt moist. I pushed my palm
against the carpeting, and water sloshed between my fingers.
An old copper water pipe had snapped in the guest bathroom,
flooding our downstairs.

That's when we filed our first insurance claim and discovered what most homeowners already know: after the deductible,
the insurance company only assumes responsibility for restoring
the damaged area to preflood conditions. But if we orchestrated
the repairs ourselves and covered the additional costs, we could
provide a much-needed update to our 1970s-style basement.

Skimming online ads, I found a licensed, bonded repairman
named Bruce who provided competitive prices and outstanding
references that we carefully checked. He promised completion
of work in three to four days. As naïve, optimistic homeowners,
we believed him.

The next day Bruce returned to our home with his friend

Allen. The work took longer than anticipated. A few days became a week. A week rolled into two. Then three. Then four. Then five. Would the project ever end?

Along the way, we started to piece together their story. Bruce and Allen were both ex-felons. When Leif discovered this tidbit, he shared details of the years he had spent working with the federal government in security. I still don't know the details, but after that conversation they proceeded to refer to Leif as "Marshall" and called me "Ma'am" for the rest of their time with us.

One day Bruce approached Leif about borrowing a hair dryer. *That's a nontraditional way to dry grout,* Leif thought, but he decided to loan him one anyway. Half an hour later, Leif detected a humming sound in the garage. Bruce was using the hairdryer to peel off the marijuana stickers from the bumper of his truck. I'm still not sure if that's what Jesus meant about being salt and light.

We had to remind Bruce and Allen of the importance of keeping quiet since we worked from home. The duo was responsive in turning down their radio, but that was the only reduction in volume. In addition to the screeching of the tile saw and the banging of nails into drywall, they bickered like Jack Lemmon and Walter Matthau from *Grumpy Old Men*. To pass the time, they harmonized show tunes slightly off key. Our musical construction team was quite fond of "Circle of Life" from *The Lion King* and "Defying Gravity" from *Wicked,* ballads they belted out multiple times a day.

Bruce and Allen were with us for six noisy weeks. The repairs cost three times as much as anticipated, and by the time they left, I knew I'd never be able to get "Tomorrow" from *Annie* out of my mind.

Around the same time, several of our clients informed us that because of the changes in the economy, they simply could not fulfill their financial commitments. While we might have been able to absorb the loss at another time, our margin was already eroded from the unexpected car and home repairs. As we balanced the checkbook one night, the stress that accompanies financial overcommitment took up residence in our lives. Even though I knew in my head that God wasn't to blame, I wondered, *Why, God?*

Then I received some unexpected news. I called the doctor one day for a prescription refill. She agreed to call in the medicine to the pharmacy but suggested that I come into the office for a physical exam. I protested that I was young and didn't need one every year.

"We performed some tests last year, and the results were inconclusive," she said.

"I received a card in the mail from you that said everything was normal," I responded.

"I handwrote a note on the card," she said.

"I think I would have noticed that!" I exclaimed, attempting not to come unglued.

After scheduling an appointment, I shared the news with Leif.

"That missed note might explain some things going on in your body," he said.

Sometimes I joke with friends that I'm like Dory from *Finding Nemo,* who suffers from short-term memory loss. I'm known to lose my sunglasses on top of my head and call myself dozens of time a day to relocate my ever-lost cell phone. I'm the most forgetful in regards to my body. Over the last few years I've grown accustomed to various foods making me ill and learned to push through all the moments I don't feel well. Even if I notice the discomfort or sickness, I don't remember it for very long.

But Leif had been noticing some disturbing symptoms: namely, that I felt crummy more days than I felt strong. I'd developed a bright red spot in my right eye that the ophthalmologist's prescriptions couldn't alleviate, everyday scratches and scrapes were taking longer to heal, and I'd been bleeding for months.

"What if all these symptoms are all connected?" he asked.

"That's silly," I protested. "I'm fine."

As hard as I tried to muster the forgetfulness of Dory, the words hung suspended in my mind.

My appointment with the physician arrived. After a short discussion, she confessed, "Something is wrong, but I don't know what it is. You need to see a specialist."

She failed to offer the answer or the reassuring words I longed for. The most highly recommended doctor in our area didn't have an opening for weeks. I seesawed between hope and despair with each passing day. Online research only expanded my fears.

The meeting with the specialist included a physical exam and blood work performed in-office. When the doctor returned, she spoke all too familiar words: "Something is wrong, but I don't know what it is."

"Do I have cancer?"

"I don't know," she said. "You need to go see the doctor who writes the textbook on this."

Despite a personal call from the doctor, the super-specialist's first available date was more than a month out. I left the office feeling hollow and tinny as if everything inside was vacuumed away. When I returned home, I crawled into bed where I tossed and turned until I lay sweaty and laboring for breath.

I trudged through the next few days trying to hold together some shred of sanity, some peanut of productivity. Then the phone rang. A dear friend had died unexpectedly. I felt as if I'd been battered by life then sucker punched. I couldn't help but wonder why.

Any one of the events—transmission repair, house flooding, financial pressures, health issues, or death of a loved one—was challenging yet manageable, but when they all aligned together in such a short time, I found myself overpowered by the shock and awe.

That's when I collapsed on my kitchen floor and rolled to my back, stretching my hands above the top of my head. Crumbs, like sand, ground against my limbs. Pressed against the hardwood flooring, I felt the presence of God's Spirit—that very thing I'd been asking for—grip me. I discovered a holy stanza emerging from the recesses of my soul. My lips began trembling. My eyes searched the ceiling as the whisper of these words ascended from the core of my being.

God is good.
God is on the throne.
Breathe in.
Breathe out.[1]

I finished the refrain then returned to the beginning.

Some say it's impossible to rediscover something for the first time. Maybe they're right. But in that moment I felt as if these simple truths were familiar and foreign all at the same time.

In those dozen syllables, I discovered I wasn't only speaking to God; he was speaking to me—anchoring me to the reality of his immanence. That's when God filled me with the wonder of his presence. God wasn't just with me on the kitchen floor; he had been with me all along. God's presence had never left. I had been so focused on the areas of pain, the problems that seemed to have no end, that I was missing out on the nearness of God in the moment.

The wonder of God's presence captured me. A ripple of peace brushed against my soul. A wave of joy crashed over me that I could not contain. Rolling laughter erupted from my belly: I found myself delighting in the invisible and unexplainable assurance that God was near. For the first time in months, I felt alive. In a jubilant response, laid out on the kitchen floor, I traced an upward arc with my hands until my knuckles bumped then pushed my arms back down toward my sides. My legs joined the cadence. My limbs swung in rhythm as I offered God a spontaneous act of worship by making snow angels on the kitchen floor.

I knew I looked ridiculous. My response made no sense. Laughter marks the last response a sane person makes to pain. But the wonder I discovered that day is that when God feels a million miles away, the knowledge of his presence allows us to laugh when everything else says we should be crying. In such a moment, I couldn't help but respond in worship.

Wide awake to the presence of God, I realized I had been so focused on asking why a good God allowed bad things to happen that I was missing out on the nearness of God all along. In becoming preoccupied with the *why*, I was missing the *who*.

Over the following days, I began returning to Scripture to find God anew. I discovered that the subtle but significant shift taking place in my life echoes throughout the Bible.

While taking care of the sheep of his father-in-law Jethro, Moses stumbles on a fiery bush that refuses to burn up. When he turns aside to find out why the shrub isn't reduced to ashes, he encounters the holy *who* that changes his life and the history of the Israelites.[2]

God instructs Moses to demand that Pharaoh, the ruler of Egypt, set the Israelites free. Moses obeys but becomes disappointed and disillusioned at the response. Instead of granting liberation, Pharaoh doubles the workload. Moses bombards God with a series of why questions: "O Lord, *why* have You brought harm to this people? *Why* did You ever send me?"[3]

Instead of answering Moses' questions of *why*, God responds to Moses' questions with *who*. Just as God revealed himself in increasing measure to Abraham, Isaac, and Jacob, God promises to reveal himself to Moses and the Israelites. He fulfills the commitment with spectacular fanfare. Water becomes blood. Insects multiply. Clouds thunder. Hail descends. Darkness falls. The Red Sea splits. Manna appears. Water pours from a rock. And that's only the beginning.

The winding dusty path from Egypt to the promised land proves to be far more than a much-needed shift in geography or transition from slavery to liberation; the great exodus is a journey in discovering the presence of God anew. Abounding love. Generous provision. Exceptional patience. Miraculous power.

Sporting chapped lips and sunburnt noses, the people of God discover the nature of God with each passing mile. They grumble ten thousand complaints and ask unending *why* questions. They even endure consequences, some harsh at times, because of their disobedience and lack of faith. Yet God still meets them in the *who*.

This idea of God answering our *why* questions with the holy *who* isn't just seen in the history of the Israelites but is also displayed in the story of a wildly successful businessman named Job who, in a single day, loses everything.

A rogue storm smashes the home where Job's children gather for a party. A bolt of lightning strikes the barn nearby, leaving all his sheep and shepherds trapped in a fire. With smoke still billowing, looters arrive on the scene. They cart away all of Job's remaining livestock. By the time law enforcement and rescue workers arrive, everything is gone. Almost everyone is dead.

The calamities continue. Job's body breaks out in painful boils. Sitting in the dusty ashes of a life destroyed, he scrapes his skin with smashed pottery shards to alleviate the pain. Job prays to die, but his broken heart refuses to stop beating. Looking into the eyes of the woman he loves, he finds himself longing for a droplet of hope, a splash of encouragement. Instead, she advises him to curse God and grab a noose. The responses of Job's friends, Eliphaz, Bildad, and Zophar, prove even more disheartening. Though the trio of theological quacks can't pinpoint which sin Job has committed to cause all of this, Job maintains his innocence.

Instead of responding in anger frosted with bitterness, Job

declares no luggage racks are allowed on the hearse. He came into the world with nothing; he will return with nothing. Regardless of what he gives or takes away, Job proclaims that God still deserves praise. [4]

Job's response is curious.

He doesn't accuse God of behaving badly but peppers him with dozens of *why* questions. Why do you "kick me around like an old tin can?"[5] he asks without apology. "Why did I have to be born if this is the life you meant for me? Why do you bother keeping me alive?"[6]

The *why* dam breaks, tearful inquiries gush forth. "Why do you treat me like your enemy?"[7] Job asks. "Why don't you forgive me and move on?"[8] "Why don't you stop picking on me?"[9] "Why do you seem to ignore the wrongs of our world?"[10] In the process of calling on God for answers, Job's lament gives voice to the great whys that have plagued humanity throughout history.

He wrestles through some of life's darkest, most difficult issues. Three insufferable friends, along with an unwelcome latecomer named Elihu, weigh in at every turn. Their all-too-often barbed, coldhearted responses to Job reveal that they're more concerned with figuring out theologically what happened to him than with extending compassion. The conversation spins around issues of sin, justice, sovereignty, and mercy until God appears on the scene.

Considering all the forms God could have selected that fateful day, with burning bushes and talking donkeys not beyond reason, I find great comfort that God chooses to pull back the curtains of heaven and reveal himself in the form of a whirlwind. After a man's life has been blown apart by hurricane-force gusts and storm-tossed by well-meaning friends, God chooses to appear to him in the midst *of* a storm *as* a storm, reminding us that none of life's downpours happen apart from God's power or permission.

God assumes the form of a windstorm to deliver one of the most spectacular speeches in all of Scripture. The tenor with which God breaks the silence makes us feel like he's been holding back, holding his breath for this moment. God poses some of the finest and most fantastic questions ever asked.

Though Job asks *why*, God answers *who*. "Who developed the blueprints for the earth?"[11] he asks. "Who laid the cornerstone and poured out the foundations of creation?"[12] "Who carved the canyons to channel the rain?"[13] "Who keeps count of the clouds?"[14] "Who ensures the baby birds are well fed?[15] "Who sets the wild donkey free?"[16]

The series of questions reverberates in the soul like an ethereal ballad. The divine song raises Job's eyes from the downward and inward to the upward and outward. God asks, "Have you ever commanded the morning?"[17] and "Do you know where light dwells?"[18] Job's eyes open to the wonder of God's presence all around him.

The work of God's hand is heralded throughout creation and manifested in its many creatures. God's presence is evident in the groan of labor pains, the sweet scent of a newborn. God's handiwork is displayed in the cresting of shadows and the damp chill of morning dew. The power of God can be heard in the crackle of hail, the crash of an ocean wave, the groan of gusting wind. The nearness of God is exhibited in the daily dawn-inspired rooster's crow, the rhythmic pacing of seasons: all of creation testifies to the power and presence of God.

In the wake of such a sublime soliloquy, Job offers a final, frail question, "What else can I say?"[19] Since childhood, Job had listened to stories of God's glory and mercy and holiness and wrath. At dawn and dusk, on more days than Job could remember, he paused to admire the bright velvety colors displayed on the horizon. Even as a younger man, he watched in awe whenever one of his livestock gave birth.

Now Job hears and experiences God for himself.

After that encounter, his perspective recalibrates from a focus on the *why* to the *who*, all of his questions scuttle off, replaced by the knowledge that God had graced him with his presence. The enormity of God is revealed. Everything becomes right-sized in Job's world. Still covered in soot and scabs, Job confesses something he has known all along deep down inside: God can do anything and everything, and no one and nothing can upset the plans of God.

God meets Job in the ashes, in the midst of his lament, but God does not leave him there. In the final act, God expresses his displeasure with Job's friends and their hurtful, half-baked theology. They must humbly ask Job to make an offering and prayer on their behalf. Then, quite unexpectedly, as quickly as the tides of fortune turned against Job, they recede. God literally gives Job another lease on life; he lives to be 140 years old. Job's wealth is not only restored but doubled. Job doesn't only have more sons and daughters; he has the privilege of becoming a much-adored, great-great-grandfather.

For all that is lost and restored, Job never receives an answer to his *why*.

Yet the ancient book that bears his name allows us to press our ears against a soundproof room in the heavens to understand more. Satan, the adversary, approaches God claiming that the only reason for Job's righteousness and divine affection is because he's wealthy and prosperous. Satan argues that Job won't be faithful if stripped of his possessions. With a divine handshake, God permits Satan to strip Job of every material blessing—except his life—and an unparalleled series of catastrophic events is unleashed in Job's life.

The great irony: We get a divine peek behind the scenes, but Job never hears of the adversary's role in his ruin. Then again, maybe after Job's awakening to the presence of God all around him, the Great Who trumping every why, such details become nothing more than useless trivia.[20]

Sooner or later we all encounter situations that leave us baffled. Whether a single event or a series of circumstances that assault us with shock and awe, we're left with the unanswerable questions of why? Why me? Why now? Why again? When we ask such questions to the exclusion of all else, we can miss opportunities to encounter God in our midst. Yet the invitation to awaken the wonder all around us remains: even in the affliction, even in the loss, even in the pain, God's presence remains.

Laying hold of such wonder requires us to shift our question from *why* to *who*: *Who* will walk with me? *Who* is the source of light in my darkness? *Who* always proves faithful? As we begin asking these questions, our focus shifts from downward to upward, from inward to outward. We begin discovering the wonder of the presence of God all around us—and ultimately how he works through us. In the most opaque circumstances of life, even when he feels a million miles away, the knowledge of the presence of God allows us to laugh when everything else says we should be crying.

Do you tend to focus on the *why* or the *who* in the midst of life's challenges? What would it look like for you to pursue God in those moments when life unravels?

Though I wouldn't wish calamitous life events—whether Job-sized or more everyday—on myself or anyone else, I can't help but be wonderstruck by God's presence and faithfulness throughout my experience. The financial burden caused by the unexpected loss lessened but still remains. The grief of losing my dear friend sat heavy on my chest for some time; then one day, when I wasn't looking, it stood up and sauntered away.

Eventually the long-awaited day of seeing the super-specialist arrived. Through another series of tests and an exam, he confirmed that I didn't have cancer but a rare, mysterious disease that explained some of my symptoms. In the six-hundred-plus-page textbook he penned, this particular disease receives a meager paragraph, less than an inch of attention. A cure isn't available, but the symptoms can be somewhat managed through medication.[21]

Maybe that's why I hadn't been able to contain the deep, chesty growl of laughter as I lay on the kitchen floor, sensing what was to come. Though the *why* remained unanswered and the problems hadn't budged, I discovered that the difference between tears and laughter is found in being aware of the presence of God. Even when I lost my footing, God never stumbled. Not a single tear slipped by his sight. Not a single groan escaped his ear. I laughed for joy because in the moments when I felt most vulnerable and lost and alone and angry, God didn't shy away. In the life storms that caught me unaware, God remained all knowing. In that which took my breath away, God whispered *keep breathing*. In the holy hush of his presence, God met me.

And God will meet you there too.

.003
ALPENGLOW EVENINGS

The Wonder of Creation

NAKED WILLOWS AND WELL-CLOTHED EVERGREENS cast maroon shadows across the landscape in front of our home. The sky above, the ice below, the narrowest of tree branches—all are enveloped by a divine pinkish hue known as alpenglow. Like a checkered picnic blanket strewn across a patch of grassy earth, cotton-candy-colored snow obscures the uneven ground.

I rub my eyes this early January evening. My vision is clear. I'm not wearing rose-colored glasses. Rather, I'm encountering an optical phenomenon that occurs on rare occasions as the sun pauses below the horizon in the mountains. When rays reflect off particles such as ice, snow, and water in the lower atmosphere, they backscatter in the direction they came from, casting a licorice-red glow across the landscape.

Living in Colorado lends itself to experiencing alpenglow at dusk and daybreak, especially during the winter months. Many years ago I remember riding horses through a similar glowing scene. Cowboy Dan, who wore a bushy handlebar mustache and round wire spectacles that accentuated his sapphire eyes, asked a handful of my friends if we were interested in riding horses at his ranch in the middle of winter. With more than three feet of snow blanketing the ground, Dan assured me the horses were safe to ride year-round.

Late one afternoon, we traveled to his property, where we found Dan wearing his favorite crusty cowboy hat, stained leather chaps, and long-toed boots, still in the barn saddling the final steed.

"You'll want this one!" Dan trumpeted. "She has fire in her but not enough to get you in too much trouble."

I couldn't tell if Dan was describing the horse or making an unsolicited comment about my personality, but I detected a sly grin on his face as he clasped his hands together to form sure footing to climb into the saddle. Holding the reins, I slipped each foot into the stirrups and, with a gentle nudge, felt the animal lurch forward. My left palm clutched for stability on the saddle's horn; my right hand held onto the reins. I practiced directing the regal creature in each direction until I began to feel more balanced, more relaxed.

After Cowboy Dan gave the last member of our squadron a boost, he mounted his saddle with a smooth swinging motion. Our horses, predisposed to their own pecking order, lined up behind Dan. The clacking rhythm of hooves on the plowed gravel road complemented the cadence of our bodies rocking back and forth. We stayed on the road a quarter mile before turning onto a narrow path that led into the forest marking Dan's private property.

The unblemished snow silenced the hooves. The first shadows of dusk softened the lighting of the landscape. We entered a sacred moment in time, hushing human and animal alike. Pine tree branches bent under the weight of as much snow as they could bear. Whenever a stray stirrup or shoulder brushed against a limb, the icy flakes powdered everything in reach.

The scene of frozen beauty remained untouched except for a lone set of bunny tracks. We glimpsed a world no one else would see. My mind wandered to how many places like this God reserves for himself. From the intricacies of the solar system to the mysteries of the depths of the sea, creation radiates God's splendor in incalculable moments never perceived by any human eye. From the hidden nocturnal creatures of the desert to tucked-away flora and fauna of the tropics, they exist for God's pleasure alone. Such awareness stirred in me the longing to join creation's chorus by bringing God glory. Skirted by creation's magnificence, a song of worship crested in my soul and lifted ever so gently from my lips. Worship felt like the only response to being immersed in such sacred beauty.

My fingers stiff, my toes numb from the cold, I still wanted to savor every last sip of the surrounding beauty. The trail zigzagged through the forest before vanishing into an unmarred snowy meadow shaded in alpenglow. The last few rays of daylight cast a hue of pink champagne across the landscape. On the far edge of the open field, the red barn where we'd begun our journey stood radiant against the snow.

"Anyone want to see what their horse can really do?" yelled Cowboy Dan, still leading the lineup.

In unison, we hooted and hollered. I pressed my toes tight into the stirrups, lifting my body above the saddle, before administering a swift kick. The horse began to trot. Another nudge and the stately animal pressed into a full-fledged gallop as if swallowing freedom with each lunge forward. Snow scattered in all directions. Cold air stung my face. My eyes watered. Yet I felt wholly alive, as if I were pressing my fingertips against the heavens. Approaching the barn, I tugged back on the reins and, caught, my, breath. Pausing before dismounting the horse, I realized if I had stayed home or declined the invitation, I would have missed this magnificence.

The snowy field outside our home looks different than the one we raced across years ago. Tracks from the deer and footprints from neighborhood kids who spent all afternoon constructing a crooked snowman crisscross the landscape. But the intoxicating pink hue is almost the same.

Admiring the beauty, I consider how many holy moments I've missed in the harriedness of life. Though God laces creation with eternal truths, all too often I pass by them unaware.

Taking a walk in a nearby park on a spring Sabbath afternoon, I follow the path along the riverbank. Towering trees line the path, their leafy branches chattering and clattering. Distracted by the ruckus of my life, I miss the holy conversation: those who savor God's Word morning, noon, and night will be like a tree planted next to a stream.[1] Yet I glide by unaffected.

Looking at our lawn during the summer, I'm reminded of the stubble left behind after our grass is mowed. Within a few days, the trimmings fade like blanched almonds, leaving an abstract pattern on our lawn. The sun-cured grass prevents the young shoots from surviving, so I scurry back and forth across the front yard pocketing the remains in a garbage bag. Each clenched handful produces a soft crunching and scrunching, but in my hurry, I miss the eternal truth in my grasp: the withering grass alludes to the brevity of life—make the most of every God-given day.[2]

Or those rainy fall days when I'm homebound by what feels like an eternal storm. With each plop and plunk, the raindrops dimple the glassy surface of my windows, obscuring the view. I interpret the loud rooftop pitters and patters as proudly announcing all the things I won't be able to do today, tomorrow, or the next—until the rain ends. The list makes me feel imprisoned, isolated, ineffective. Like the blurred glass, I can't see clearly. I misunderstand the sacred message of all those pitter-patters telling me that if I paused long enough, I'd discover the splashing rain was shouting, jumping, beckoning me toward the cleansing

I needed—not only on my rooftop or windows but also in my heart.[3]

Scripture affirms that God speaks through the chattering and clattering, crunching and scrunching, pittering and pattering, yet I've been unresponsive.

The scientific community is also discovering the outdoors as a divine elixir. Researchers at the University of Michigan determined that participants' memory performance and attention spans improved by 20 percent after an hour of interacting with nature. They also discovered the benefits of the outdoors were the same whether the temperature was 80 degrees and sunny or 25 degrees and frigid—though the study acknowledged participants enjoyed exercising outdoors more in the late spring than the middle of winter.[4]

Scientists in Sweden found that joggers who exercise in settings with trees and landscape views felt more rejuvenated and wrestled with fewer bouts with anxiety, anger, or depression than those who completed the same exercise regimen in an urban setting.[5] And Australian researchers believe the sudden skyrocket in nearsightedness—myopia—among youth is due to young people spending less time outdoors where their eyes learn to focus on longer distances.[6]

I recently stumbled on the groundbreaking book by conservationist Richard Louv, *The Nature Principle*, which explores these studies and many more. Louv points out that for the first time in history, more than half of the world's population lives in towns and cities rather than more rural environments. The traditional ways humans interacted with creation are disappearing. As we enter the age of electronic connectivity, we're becoming less connected to our natural environment. The result is that many of us are suffering from nature-deficit disorder, which he defines as "an atrophied awareness, a diminished ability to find meaning in the life that surrounds us, whatever form it takes."[7] He argues this reduction in our lives has a direct impact on our physical, mental, and societal health.

Reflecting on Louv's definition and studies from the scientific community, I can't help but think "atrophied awareness" also affects our spiritual lives. We know time in the outdoors affects our physical bodies. When we leave our cubicles and step into nature, the environment demands that we hone our senses. We must gauge depth perception, utilize peripheral vision, respond to instinct, and finely tune *proprioception*, the awareness of our body's position through balance and movement—physical engagements that lie dormant whenever we become mouse potatoes, spending day after day and week upon week staring at a computer screen.

But what about atrophied spiritual awareness? What if the reduction in time spent outdoors impacts our relationship with God and the restorative work he wants to do in our lives?

Spending time outdoors has a way of shifting our perspective from inward to outward as we see the delicacies and intricacies of God's creation. From the sun-bleached sandy beaches of the coast to the seemingly endless plains, we capture snapshots of God's power and precision, his connectedness and intimate care. One of the great wonders of creation is that God uses our natural world to alert us to his presence.

From the opening pages of Genesis, God reveals his nature—in nature. The story of creation broadcasts the distinctiveness of our God as the source of life. All-powerful, wildly creative, infinitely wise, God is the supreme ruler. His throne isn't founded in suspicion or threat but blessing and celebration. Creation divulges the goodness of God as he declares the good, good, good of creation.

Unlike other religions attempting to find guidance amidst the stars of the sky or the fear of the unknown, our God hangs stars, slings comets, and designs sea creatures. Apart from him, they do not exist. In the face of blackness and chaos, our God speaks illumination and order. As the pinnacle of all he makes, God handcrafts humanity in his own image, entrusts us with dominion, and insignias us for relationship with himself.

Sitting in the darkness of a sky turned wholly to night, I speculate: if God spoke creation into existence, should we be surprised when creation speaks back to us about God?

The sights surround us. The sounds summon us. The wonder of creation beckons.

Scripture sparkles resplendent with such moments, remind-ing us that creation is a live theater that invites us to experience and comprehend God more. The psalmist reminds us God's faithfulness is woven into the canopy of the heavens,[8] his loving-kindness displays itself throughout the earth.[9] The subterranean depths of the ocean speak of the wisdom of God's judgments,[10] and the horizons herald how far God removes our sins.[11] God's rule reveals itself in day, night, and seasons: his voice rumbles in the thunder.[12]

On the days we begin to question God's power or sover-eignty, the psalmist points to the hail, fire, wind, and snow as elements that obey God's command.[13] In the moments we start to question God's saving grace, the psalmist recalls the miracles of salvation in the sea and storm to remind us no one resides beyond God's rescue.[14]

Creation's comparisons provide firm warnings against self-destructive and foolish behavior. Scoffers are like empty grain husks, and those who lack understanding like stubborn mules.[15] Egomaniacs who overestimate themselves are billowing clouds that never produce rain,[16] and it's better to encounter a mama bear robbed of her cubs than a fool.[17]

The psalmist alludes to God's tenderheartedness and teachings tucked into creation when describing the place a barn swallow finds to lay her eggs.[18] Picturing the scene makes me smile. One day, a mother bird searches for a secure place to build a home. The bird finds a crevice near the altar where the burnt offerings of the temple are consumed and begins the process of building a mud nest. She darts to a nearby water source that provides the much-needed moist firmament and shapes the first mudball in her mouth. With the help of her monogamous mate, they build a cup-shaped home piece by piece with more than a thousand small balls.

I speculate: when the religious leaders caught on to the birds' construction plans, did any of them propose moving the nest?

The scripture doesn't say. Instead, Psalm 84 celebrates that blessing befalls everyone who dwells in the house of the Lord—even the birds! From their nooks and from their crannies, the winged creatures join the chorus of worship in the temple. The choice imagery reminds us the invitation to reside with God extends to everyone. Those who choose to respond will find fellowship with a God who sees, hears, cares, and provides.

Centuries after the psalmist penned these lines, Jesus used these little creatures to remind his followers that God takes great care with winged creatures. Though they don't plant or reap or store harvests in barns, God feeds them. If God's care and provision is so generous for a bird, how much more generous will God be with us? Jesus notes that a single sparrow doesn't die without God attending the funeral. If God cares so much for these creatures, how much more does God care for us?[19]

Such realities provide insights into the Creator and his infinite wisdom. Maybe that's one reason the outdoors is so rejuvenating. The sky, the land, the vegetation, the animals all speak of the power, the majesty, the goodness of God. They remind us of God's presence in our world, strengthening our faith, comforting our soul, and encouraging us to continue pursuing him. The vastness of creation trumpets God's transcendence and immanence—allowing us to bask in the wonder of both God's enormity and infinitesimal intricacy.

For me, spending time in creation is a portal to connect with God. Almost every day, I spend an hour walking the trails around our home. The seasoned paths provide an opportunity for me to recalibrate my mind, emotions, and body as thoughts sprout and creativity blossoms.

On that unforgettable evening of horseback riding years ago, the sky held a pinkish red hue much the same color as I see tonight. Both then and on this night, I've been arrested by the wonder of creation—moments that stir my hunger to know God more.

If God creates such exquisiteness, how much more magnificent is the Creator? Even the most spectacular displays in the cosmos only hint at the splendor of God; the deepest insights into nature are shallow observations compared to the depth of the nature of God. Creation awakens me to God, inviting me to attune my senses to his presence and voice.

The wonder of creation is every encounter illuminates something about God. He is the One who formed distant galaxies and our tender planet, and the fullness of creation belongs to him. God utilizes elements of creation to witness to his invisible attributes and character.

The mesmerizing beauty through my window leaves me breathless. I purse my lips and inhale mouthfuls of much-needed oxygen. All too soon, the color sharpens into rubies. I feel aglow.

Such beauty creates within me an aching, a longing deep within and far beyond myself. I sense the warmth that follows any significant encounter with the handiwork of God. I don't want to move. Too many months have passed since I tasted such divine delicacy. Instead of looking for the holy glimpses in the dawn, the dusk, and everywhere between, I've slept through far too many of such moments. But tonight, God cast ten thousand rose petals across the landscape to awaken me to himself.

I'm wonderstruck that God will use everything from a winter horseback ride to the hues of the setting sun to draw us toward himself.

Have you awakened to the wonder of God in creation? Have you considered setting your alarm earlier to capture a sunrise or set an alarm in the evening so you don't miss the sun dipping below the horizon? Will you trade moments in front of the computer for time in creation, maybe spending your lunch hour in a park, serenaded by birdsong and breeze? Will you develop rhythms in your life that foster spiritual vitality and a greater awareness of God?

Staring out my window, I can still make out the icy blanket

on the field below. The pomegranate tone fades to wild strawberries before vanishing into a deep slate grey. The first star appears in the night sky.

Through the beauty of alpenglow, I'm reminded of the foundational truth that God is light.[20] I'm acutely aware of my need for God, the Great Luminary, to shimmer the miracle of light in me. I petition: *God, illuminate the hidden parts of my soul still dwelling in darkness. Brighten the areas of my life where I still cling to shadows. Soften the light through which I see others. Help me be a luminary of you. Amen.*

.004:
A SANCTUARY
IN TIME

The Wonder of Rest

SPEEDING THROUGH LIFE AT WHAT I BELIEVED was a healthy pace, I ran out of gas without as much as a flicker from the fuel warning light. I completed projects and checked off to-do lists without hesitation until I woke up one Monday feeling like a ghost of my former self, hollow and faintly present.

The shift in disposition was noticeable. With a Tigger-like personality, most mornings I bounce out of bed ready to conquer the world. Suddenly I felt like the world had conquered me. At two in the afternoon, still wearing holiday cherry-red and lime-green flannel pajamas that should have long been packed away, I confessed my emptiness to Leif.

"I can't do this anymore," I said.

"Let's take the rest of the day off," he advised. "We'll crawl into bed and watch movies all afternoon."

"I don't think you heard me," I clarified. "I *really* can't do this anymore."

A quick self-inventory suggested something deep down inside was broken. It wasn't that I couldn't stomach another deadline, though I sat before a stack of projects. Or that I wasn't sleeping well, though I tried everything I knew to sleep through the night. Or that I felt smothered by the onslaught of demands that popped into my inbox each day. Or that I sensed the shallowness of being consumed by a hundred meaningless activities. Or that I could no longer shove away the isolation that comes from being only partially present to everyone in my life—including God.

My heart felt singed around the edges. Everyday challenges seemed insurmountable. I struggled to find the energy to care, let alone attempt to change the situation. Anxiety and frustration amassed until I felt trapped; in the darkness, I saw no way of escape.

I knew I needed to talk to someone who could pinpoint the source of my exhaustion, but I cringed with feelings of embarrassment and shame. Would the admission that I needed help certify that I was permanently broken, disturbed, losing my mind?

I disregarded the voices of disgrace. With the assistance of a friend, I found a Christian counseling center. Leif and I drove to the first session together. As we pulled into the parking lot, I discovered, much to my chagrin, I'd be sorting through my emotional baggage at a strip mall. The walls of the tiny offices held a few watercolor paintings, the rooms plainly decorated with a mishmash of home décor, the most notable piece a basket of faded silk flowers. Every bookshelf jammed tight with books, the office smelled like animal crackers—which turned out to be the complimentary afternoon snack. The counselor invited me to have a seat on the dilapidated black leather couch. I chuckled at the stereotype.

Leif sat beside me during each session, adding insights as the counselor prodded me to unpack my childhood, adolescence, and current situation. We didn't leave a topic unexplored—no hope, no dream, no disappointment. The first day was largely uneventful, but halfway through the second, the counselor said something that sparked me like an electric current.

"Margaret, you don't have any boundaries," he told me.

"That's not true," I protested. "Everyone has some boundaries or we'd all run around naked eating cheeseburgers all the time."

The counselor offered a big loopy grin before breaking into a laugh, infusing the conversation with much-needed levity.

"Well, yes, we all have some boundaries, but do you realize you don't have any *healthy* boundaries?" he asked.

Running through the various categories of my life, including work, friends, family, and free time, I knew he was right.

"Have you heard of the book *Boundaries* by Henry Cloud and John Townsend?" he asked.

"I've read it twice," I answered.

"Great," he said. "But you haven't put a single thing they've written into practice."

I had my work cut out for me—not just because I was required to watch two hours of *Boundaries* lectures per night in addition to finishing mounds of homework but also because the new terrain of learning to say no was foreign, steep, and downright scary. The counselor roused me, asking me to become alert to the work God wanted to do in my life; I responded with hesitance, wishing I could roll over, pull the blanket over my head, make everything go away. Despite my reluctance, I awakened to the harsh truth that developing a healthy sustainability for life was as much a mystery to me as string theory.

We discussed my upbringing during the sessions together. I began to notice a pattern. My inability to create margins traced back to my childhood in Cocoa Beach, Florida, where my parents owned a mom-and-pop surf shop. They stayed busy advising customers on the best choice among surfboards, rehanging bikinis, and managing quirky employees. I learned early on that owning your own business required extra hours on the job. Working every day of the week, more than a dozen hours a day, was standard procedure. To balance their work ethos, my parents developed a habit of taking extended breaks to escape on a boat where they sailed away from the relentless demands of the surf shop. This upbringing taught me to never be afraid of a hard day's work or a long day's play.

Along the way, I failed to develop healthy life rhythms. Many find the workplace provides an opportunity to practice establishing good personal borders, but I chose to follow in my parents' footsteps as an entrepreneur. To make matters worse, I adored my work and found great satisfaction in my job. Instead of learning to saunter through life at a sustainable pace, I lunged forward at breakneck speeds that left me worn, weary, and winded.

The pace of life became a place of torment. My life was a smoking treadmill I'd been running on at level ten speed at an incline of ten since childhood. I didn't know anything different. This explained why I felt so tired and trapped—why even after eight hours of sleep I still woke up exhausted, why the smallest demands of life loomed large, why I felt stuck without any reprieve, why I had awakened feeling like a faint wisp of my former self.

Sitting in the counselor's office, my emotions felt like an oil fire with smoke billowing everywhere. My red-hot reaction was to smash what had driven me into a thousand pieces, but I knew that sooner or later I'd find a replacement. Freedom wasn't found in tossing the treadmill, but in discovering a maintainable pace. Suggesting this to the counselor, he smiled for a second time.

When I had become passionate about the need for downtime in short stints, the demands of life always wore down my determination. Like slicing a Honeycrisp apple extra thin to enjoy it longer, whatever time I set apart for respite was cut in half then reduced to quarters, then eighths, and finally sixteenths until any satisfying sense of sweet nourishment disappeared.

Though God had been echoing the invitation to enter his rest, I hesitated to respond because somewhere along the journey of life I had developed a mangled perspective. For me, downtime felt like detention: a forced confinement in which I was restrained against my will. I viewed respite like a tether holding me back rather than a resilient spring propelling me into the fullness of life God intended. As a result, I spent a lifetime outrunning downtime and missing out on one of the greatest wonders of all: rest.

The counselor challenged my distorted view. Through our discussions I came to see rest as a divine invitation to make the physical, emotional, and spiritual confession that God is Lord of all. If I affirm that God holds everything together, then I'm free to establish a sustainable rhythm as I entrust everything and everyone to God. When I enter into God's rest, I crawl into bed knowing the world lounges safely in his hands.

But the biggest epiphany came when I realized that apart from the divine gift of downtime I cannot fully awaken to the presence of God. Rest refreshes our physical bodies, expands our mental capacities, and increases our spiritual awareness. Yet I had slept through some of God's most spectacular displays because I failed to rest.

With this wondrous discovery beating in my heart—a

lack of rest makes me drowsy to God's presence—I desperately wanted to awake. Staring at the counselor, I begged him to tell me what to do. He advised me to take responsibility: The pace of my life was my making, and only I could undo it. The grassy meadows and still waters described in the Twenty-third Psalm awaited, but I had to choose to answer the invitation of the Good Shepherd.

I stepped out of the strip mall dazed by the moment of discovery as well as all the work I had to do. Entering God's rest required more than taking a catnap or pressing snooze—I had to become deliberate and intentional about the way I lived. That evening Leif and I discussed what it meant, not just for me, but for us, to unwrap the gift of rest in our lives. We needed to develop life-giving rhythms, a sustainable pace. Our approach to everyday life required a change.

We committed to realigning our lives. We woke up earlier, added exercise to our regimen, and reset our mealtimes. The tipping point: when we both committed to finish work by 6:00 p.m. and established a reasonable bedtime. Adjusting to the fledgling schedule, we found ourselves becoming more rested and fully present.

Secretly, I hoped to be as productive working nine hours as fourteen and struggled to accept smaller yields of accomplishment at the end of each day. Limiting my time at work meant reducing the number of projects I took on. For the first few months, I swung like a broken sprinkler head toward extremes.

I said no to everything—including some things I should have said yes to—but slowly discovered a more balanced approach. I gauged potential participation in everyday activities with the knowledge that every yes costs me three nos. My daily decisions soon became more thoughtful, intentional, prayerful. I wasn't just giving myself; I was giving my *best* self to my relationships and work.

With rest, I noticed God-moments I might have missed before. My prayers grew clearer. Studying the Scripture became more meaningful. When life was rushed, I felt like I was reading a cookbook backward—nothing connected or made sense. Now I felt more attuned to God's voice in the Bible.

Sometimes you have to slow to a stop and reset before you can experience divine presence. My hunger to know God increased as I learned to develop a healthy rhythm in life and rediscovered the wonder of rest.

Like a great comet catapulted across a starry night, God's holy encore awed me. All the adjustments in daily life prepared me to rediscover one of the most beautiful gifts: Sabbath. This delightful treat of God isn't one he keeps to himself but shares freely with humanity. God established the Sabbath from the beginning of time for all time. In a world marked by endless demands to work and produce, God issues an invitation to rest. Scholars debate which came first, the word *Sabbath*—or *Shabbat*, as it's known in Hebrew—or the word *ceasing*," since *Shabbat* is derived from the Hebrew word *sh-b-t*, meaning "to cease." Regardless, the primary meaning of Sabbath reminds us that if we do not master the art of ceasing, we cannot master the art of rest.

Making time to pause isn't just a holy opportunity but a divine command. Despite studying one of the most important ritual observances in Judaism and listening to dozens of teachings on its importance, the Sabbath had remained a negotiable in my life. I treated the Sabbath like a rainy day fund, convincing myself that a single cloud justified a withdrawal. The Sabbath became a time bank to purchase all kinds of things I couldn't afford the other six days of the week. I thought I could draw on the account as much as I needed, any time I needed, without consequence. Not until I woke up and confessed, *I can't do this anymore*, did I realize all of my withdrawals had left me bankrupt.

I restudied the Sabbath in Scripture in the weeks following counseling. After an unforgettable encounter with God on Mount Sinai, Moses delivers the Ten Commandments to the Israelites. Of all the edicts, I chose to be the most deliberate in breaking the longest one. While many of the commandments are short and direct, like "Don't murder" and "Don't steal," Moses spells out what it means to honor the Sabbath, highlights acceptable behavior, and even offers a brief history of the day's importance, alluding to God's affections for humanity.

The only other place where Moses becomes as long-winded is the second commandment, which forbids idolatry, maybe because failure to rest, like idolatry, supplants God with lesser affections. Moses pauses to emphasize the ease with which we can find ourselves ascribing value to anything and everything other than God. At times we'll be tempted to construct our own idols, but despite their appeal and allure, attributing worth to anything other than God comes at great cost. The forbidding of idols isn't meant to detain us from something good but to protect us from something destructive, spotlighting the breadth of God's love.

Though I had always seen these two commands as separate in the past, I now viewed them as walking hand in hand. Apart from developing a healthy rhythm of rest, we succumb to idols and their constant demands. The Sabbath provides the space we need to recognize the false gods that slip into our lives when we're distracted. This holy day gives us the opportunity to remove them and recalibrate our lives to God.

The Sabbath roots us in God's love for us and for all of creation. In Exodus 20:10, Moses describes the Sabbath as a day when everyone, including our family, friends, employees, and guests—even our animals—should cease from work. In essence, the blessing and sanctity of the day should overflow to everyone we know, everything we touch. Behind the command is the ferocious love of God that reminds us we were never meant for slavery or exploitation. Simply put: in the process of honoring the Sabbath, we learn to treat people better. We have the opportunity to celebrate their work and rest and play and spiritual growth—not just our own.

Moses notes that the Sabbath finds its roots in Genesis—the story of creation where God is revealed as one who celebrates the good, the *tov*, of creation with a rhythm as natural as exhaling. With each passing day, the heavens and earth splash to life until the sixth day, when God declares the forming of humanity as *tov me'od*, or abundantly good. The work of creation is a good and purposeful work performed by a good and purposeful God.

Of all the days, perhaps the seventh is the most eloquent and insightful as to the nature of God. From a literary perspective, the Sabbath forms the pinnacle of the story. Like the dramatic kiss of a soldier returning from war, this is the moment we're not meant to miss. In choosing rest as the grand finale, God reveals himself as one driven by neither anxiety nor fear but one who finds gladness in both the work of creation and the creation of work.

On the Sabbath, the world rests firmly in the palms of God. Neither the stars nor the birds fall from the sky. But unlike the other days of creation, the entry is missing the closing refrain, "And there was evening and there was morning the [insert the numeral] day."[1] All other days close with the same chorus, except the seventh. Why? Maybe because God is inviting us to enter rest and reminding us that the invitation has no expiration date.

This scriptural detail is a source of great comfort, because it means that no matter how many times we reduce the Sabbath to nothing more than an hour of church or five minutes of shut-eye or another long day of hard work or play, the invitation to enter the rest of God has no end. The Sabbath is a sanctuary in time with doors that remain wide open—even for the bankrupt like me.

If we choose to enter, we may find ourselves partaking of the very sustenance of God.

During the first few weeks of remembering the Sabbath, I reminded myself of this truth as I struggled to break old habits. Innocently popping online to research a recipe or factoid, I'd get lost in hours of work e-mails. Opening a book for leisure, I'd end up outlining a possible magazine article for work. Even during an afternoon with friends, the conversation circled back to work. Celebrating the wonder of rest on the Sabbath turned out to be more difficult than I imagined. But also filled with rich rewards.

A Jewish philosopher once made the keen observation that the Sabbath isn't for the sake of the other days of the week, but the other days of the week are for the sake of the Sabbath. This great day isn't an interlude but the climax of living.[2] Through the Sabbath, God asks us to slow down so we once again become awestruck by the goodness of God in our lives, relationships, and world. The Sabbath provides the opportunity to nurture our appreciation for the beauty of creation, the deliciousness of provision, the joy of celebration. In a single day, God gives us the opportunity to recapture the wonder of everyday life.

A full day of rest forced me to develop a hybrid of passive and active events that are truly life giving:

A late morning walk.

A handful of scriptures for reflection.

A church gathering.

A book read in pinches throughout the day.

A meal with dear friends.

An afternoon nap.

An early bedtime.

I discovered the Sabbath isn't about what is done or left undone as much as breathing in the goodness of God. The more I inhaled, the more I desired another long breath.

Setting apart one day each week required forethought. Sometimes it's easy to read the story of creation and think that on the seventh day God's work was done, but really God's work had only just begun. Yet God chose to break anyway. That's an important detail because on the evening before the Sabbath I, too, discover how much more could be done. I can't run headfirst into the Sabbath sanctuary and expect to find deep spiritual replenishment; rather, I've had to learn how to develop a relaxed stroll. Slowing my pace has to begin a day or two before as I make sure the house is relatively clean, the dryer empty, the clothes semi-neatly folded so these chores don't niggle at me during the day of rest.

One Sabbath lingers in my mind as especially meaningful. I awoke that morning, crawled out of bed, and opened the blinds before nestling back in bed with a long s-t-r-e-t-c-h. Through the window, I imbibed the beauty of the indigo sky. Expressions of worship and adoration naturally flowed as I reflected on God's goodness. I lay in the stillness for some time before following the sweet tangy scent of simmering green chili into the kitchen. Lifting the lid of the Crock-Pot, I inhaled the zesty deliciousness. Then I plucked a tangerine from the fruit bowl and joined Leif on the living room couch where he shared the details of a zany dream from the night before involving Secret Service agents and a speedboat. We chatted for some time before becoming absorbed in reading—he dove into his book on the fear of the Lord while I relished a commentary on the Gospel of John.

The allure of the green chili chicken became irresistible.[3] With the meal prepared the day before, cooking on the Sabbath becomes an option rather than necessity. I heated a handful of white corn tortillas. We sat gathered around our kitchen table to eat and pray. Then we both took time to engage in life-giving activities. Our choices couldn't be more different. Leif caught up with friends on PlayStation; I reflected and prayed during a long hike. That evening we gathered in the kitchen for another round of chili before watching a light-hearted comedy together.

The Sabbath is a reflection of so many attributes and characeristics of God—his love, goodness, wisdom, holiness, and sovereignty to name just a few. Through Sabbath, I rediscover God as the source of peace amid activity, the source of quiet in the noise, the sustainer of my soul. Though this particular day wasn't marked by any spiritual epiphany or profound moments, when I crawled into bed that evening, I sensed the sweet smile of God on my life. In Sabbath, I unwrapped the culmination of the good gifts God had been longing for me to experience all along. In a mere twenty-four hours, God enhanced everything from my perspective to my energy level to my appreciation of others. The day renewed my joy in the beautiful gift of God called life.

Sabbath became an extension of the rhythm of rest God was working into every area of my life. This weekly spiritual practice shifted from a negotiable to a non-negotiable—a holy moment when I practiced establishing healthy boundaries with myself, others, and God. At times I still struggle to distinguish between the borders of work and play and rest. I accidentally bump the up arrow rather than the down arrow on the treadmill. But the mistakes I make one day can be redeemed the next.

Looking back on the transformation that came through choosing to embrace rest, I'm shocked that such small changes could have such an enormous impact. Yet they're changes that almost anyone can make. We can choose to develop a healthy rhythm and learn to embrace the wonder of rest. Such rhythms of rest will look different for everyone—especially when it comes to the Sabbath.[4]

Such shifts begin with an honest personal inventory: In what areas of your life do you need to learn to say no? Where are you prone to overcommit and overextend? What healthy rhythms do you need to establish in your work, relationships, and daily schedule—including the Sabbath—to seize the life God has for you?

One day, some four months later, I woke up feeling something I hadn't for as long as I could remember: I felt alive—my mind clear, my imagination ignited, my senses attuned to possibilities all around me. Joy percolated in my soul. My internal energy tank splashed over the rim. Life became manageable.

I felt like I had something to give again.

My eyes still adjusting to the morning sun, I felt a smile saunter across the corners of my face. I turned to Leif and whispered in his ear, "I'm not tired anymore."

.005:
FORGOTTEN
LONGINGS

The Wonder of Prayer

SOME ANGLICAN FRIENDS, wearing soot on their foreheads, introduced me to Lent more than a decade ago. Until then, my faith tradition was decidedly non-liturgical, and such attentiveness to the church calendar was new to me. From their descriptions, I imagined Lent as a formidable character who rode into town each year on the eve of Ash Wednesday and stayed until Easter morning. He spent every waking moment petitioning believers to prepare for Holy Week through a blend of prayer, repentance, giving, and self-denial. Though noble, Lent was dismissed with barely a glance. I treated him as if he were a stranger at a crowded dinner party.

But Lent continued pursuing me. A group of friends sang his praises. A pastor shared with enthusiasm the difference Lent made in his own life. Even a few of my favorite bloggers bragged about knowing him. Each time I encountered his name, I felt like Lent was looking over my shoulder, smiling. I decided I needed to know him better.

Searching online, I studied Lent's vibrant heritage and background and read about his longtime connections with the Orthodox and Catholic churches as well as newfound friendships among Mennonites and Baptists. I discovered the roots of his name, which in Latin was *quadragesima*, meaning "fortieth" based on the forty days Jesus spent in the desert before his few brief years of earthly ministry. In the Middle Ages, he became known as Lent from a German root meaning "spring," or "long," reflective of the spring days growing in length.

The following Ash Wednesday, I knew we shared a common bond—a fiery passion for Jesus. I felt compelled to spend the next forty days studying the crucifixion and resurrection accounts in-depth. By the time Good Friday arrived, I didn't just take a fancy to Lent but also longed to know him better. My affections blossomed when I learned of Lent's passion for Christ as well as his ardor for justice as demonstrated in prayer (justice toward God), fasting (justice toward self), and almsgiving (justice toward neighbors). Charmed by his personality, I dove headfirst into the Gospels the following year for another forty days, ruminating on the life of Jesus. Lent transitioned from being a drifter passing through to a dear companion.

Forty days seemed like an expensive tithe of time when we first met, but soon our time together became as fleeting as watching tumbleweed blow across the plain on a windy day. I found myself counting down the days until Lent's homecoming by considering the best way to spend almost seven weeks together. Reflecting on the various facets of Lent's character, I debated what to give up as an act of self-denial.

My friends placed a haphazard array on the altar of oblation. Some sacrificed technological tools such as Facebook, Twitter, or texting; others gave up temptations like sugar, chocolate, caffeine, soda, or fast food. Still others committed to shrinking their carbon footprint by riding their bike more and nudging the thermostat two degrees lower. A friend even gave up porn; though an awkward announcement, I applauded his efforts and hoped they continued long past Easter.

That year I felt an overwhelming sense that God asked me to give up something rather odd: prayer.

I resisted the impulse. *Why would God ask me to give up prayer? What scripture instructs us to pray less?* The Bible implores us to pray in every situation, to never stop praying. I batted down the ridiculous thought dozens of times, but the notion returned with ever increasing velocity. With Ash Wednesday a few days away, I began asking the Lord what he meant by the idea of giving up prayer for Lent. My sense was that God didn't want me to give up *all* prayer, but lengthy prayers.

Giving in to the peculiar sacred echo, I committed to offer God only three-word prayers until Easter. The spiritual practice proved more difficult than I imagined. I could no longer thank God for this morning, because that took five words. The concept needed to be summed up in three. *Thanks, God, for this morning* became *Thanks for today.* The elementary shift in verbiage translated to a trim here, a rephrasing there, a switcheroo of words over there. Every word, every syllable, demanded mindfulness.

Most mornings I stumbled into lengthier prayers by mistake. I paused and rephrased. Then stumbled again. The painstaking process left me frustrated and edgy. Prayer times expanded, not because I felt close to God, but because crafting even a few comments took so much time.

I also recognized I'd slipped into something one of my favorite writers calls "magical religion"—those moments I convince myself I can control or conjure God through my words or actions. Though I never outwardly admitted to such practices, my new time with God exposed a deep-seated belief that if I just prayed long enough or was more articulate or heartfelt then God would answer.

While I felt free to express every need, ache, desire, and whim to God—which is essential to a true relationship—my petitions often sounded like a child's sugar-infused run-on sentences: *Dear God, thanks for this day and my husband and his parents and my parents and our one last living grandparent and our aunts and our uncles and our cousins and our second cousins and our friends and our long-distant friends and our superpup and* . . . I'd rattle on until I ran out of breath. I'd wandered across the invisible border between prayer and rambling and needed to find my way back.

I'd lost sight of God as a loving Father—whose favor I didn't need to earn, whose attention I didn't need to procure; God's eyes were already on me, his hands already extended to help.[1]

The difficulty of relearning to pray lessened with each passing week. Fumbling for words dwindled whenever I used a basic breathing rhythm. When I paused for a single breath between prayers, the words rolled silky smooth rather than crunchy and coarse. The arduousness of my morning prayers eased, but I struggled to carry this newfound practice into other areas of life. Whenever Leif and I shared a meal, I would start to offer a standard blessing for our food, and Leif would gently squeeze my hand and whisper, "Three-word prayers." Even at the dinner table, I couldn't escape the tension of being intentional.

With each passing day, the process of creating three-word prayers forced me to become more engaged and creative with God. I began offering handcrafted prayers. No longer generic and mass-produced, my prayers felt artisanal.

The word *artisan* technically refers to a craftsperson or skilled worker, but in recent years, artisans and their products have been heralded as representing a departure from the mass manufactured and a return to making things by hand in small batches using time-tested methods. Artisans value personal involvement in conceiving, designing, experimenting, and creating along the way. Artisanal goods are stained with good, old-fashioned hard work and sweat.

Artisans don't just focus on the end product but the process.

Such dedication makes the difference between spongy cheap sandwich bread and a thickset, gnawy, flavorful Italian loaf made with hand-ground flour. Instead of machine-fabricated waxy chocolate, an artisan chocolatier might hike through a remote plantation in the global south to find cocoa beans to ship home, roast, and grind into the chocolate needed for dark truffles.[2]

Even the simplest items take on artisanal flair when someone cares enough about the process of creating the product. The image of the artisan illustrates much of what was taking place in my prayer life: namely, moving away from rambling, mass-produced prayers that cost me next to nothing to a richer, handcrafted prayer life. Like the artisans, I knew prayer was more than just the end product—receiving an answer from God. But I needed to be more intentional about the process. Three-word prayers required me to reengage spiritual muscles that had long ago grown flabby. These unsophisticated prayers helped me clarify my dreams and disappointments before God. With only a few words, I became more aware of what Abraham Heschel calls "the pangs we ignore, the longings we forget."[3]

These prayers ushered me into a renewed sense of openness before God. Honesty infused both my relationship with God and God's relationship with me. As our relationship became more genuine, my dependence on God increased. Throughout Lent, three-word prayers felt like I was praying with one hand and foot tied behind my back. I hobbled forward, but every movement reminded me that I wasn't getting far on my own. I needed God. Each syllable reminded me of this truth. Stripped of presumption and arrogance, of mindlessness and meaninglessness, I found myself crossing the threshold of God's domain—choosing divine will over my will and handing back what I mistook as my own. My time with God became imbued with desire and delight.

When the laborious prayers became habitual, they began to shift again. One morning, while praying for some friends whose marriage was unraveling, my request simplified.

Heal. Grace. Compassion. Reconcile. Restore.

With each word, I paused to allow the fullness of the petition to fill my being as I made the request to God. As the word *heal* rolled off my tongue, God knew I was asking for more than an end to the conflict in the couple's relationship. I petitioned for the wounds to be cleansed, bandaged, and healed. Broken bones reset. Cells regenerated. A full recovery in a single word.

With my prayer life reduced to a few syllables, every expression felt more potent than ever. Then something even more unexpected began to happen: I found myself entering a rich silence with God—the kind experienced by the closest of friends who sit side by side on a well-worn couch, feet propped up, melting into the cushions. Time slowed. The longer I sat, the less I wanted to move. Eyes grew heavy, not because of tiredness, but because I felt rested, fully myself, without any need to do anything—except be myself—in the presence of one who I love and the one I knew loved me.

Throughout my Lenten experience, I rediscovered the inward stillness of God. For years the psalmist invited me to "be still, and know that I am God," but I struggled with the continuous inner dialogue that noised up my life.[4] In this place with words nonexistent, I realized I'd been dwelling on the edge of mystery. Now I was with God in a whole new way. My soul was both nurturing and nurtured by the silence. In quelling myself, I sensed a resonance, a divine reverberation that I suspect is a facet of what the psalmist meant when he alluded to deep calling to deep.[5]

To my dismay, just as my communication with God opened again, Easter weekend approached. Watching Lent pack up felt bittersweet. The unexpected gift he brought to my prayer life made me feel melancholy about his departure, but I knew his farewell ushered in the celebration of the risen Christ.

I couldn't help but reflect on the way I had approached the forty days before Easter. I'd approached the season by asking, "What will I give up for Lent?" as if Lent's whole focus is asceticism. But Lent's concern isn't in removing something as much as receiving Someone. The passion of Lent is Christ. The annual sojourn calls for a more focused relationship with God.

Maybe instead of asking, *What are we giving up for Lent?* we need to ask, *Who and what are we trying to receive through Lent?*

As we accept this sacred solicitation with sincerity, God meets us open-armed with his goodness and grace. The transformative power of Christ awakens in our lives. The Lenten season invites us to set apart time during the beginning of each year to slough off the excess in our lives that we may live lighter and holier lives. For forty days, Lent gives us the opportunity to live in gentle receptivity of God.

After Easter, I prayed without the three-word discipline for the first time since Lent began. I waited until the house was empty and peered around the living room as if about to break a rule. I offered up a greeting. "Dear God," I whispered, "I know it's been awhile since we've spoken like this."

I began slow. The words soon picked up pace—an unculti-vated assortment of adoration and expiation, supplication and thanksgiving. Then I burst forth in prayer like a fire hydrant unplugged on a hot summer day. Conversation gushed forth from deep inside me like I was reconnecting with an old child-hood friend. I felt like I was praying—*really* praying.

When I said my final amen, I had to catch my breath. I realized why God had asked me to give up prayer for Lent: I'd been spiritually slumbering, my prayer life reduced to nothing more than sleepwalking. The Lenten season exposed all the "nonversations" in my prayer life—those moments with God where, with a litany of words, I said nothing at all. Though I spoke to God, I was half-awake at best.

God used this discipline to awaken me to the wonder of

prayer. Deliberate, uninhibited, wholly present—I found my voice with God again. I never suspected I needed to lose my prayer life in order to find it again.

From foundation to rooftop, my prayer life was undergoing major renovations, and I turned to the Scripture for a better understanding of the work God was doing in my life. I focused on the prayers of Jesus and found myself taken aback by their brevity and intentionality. Jesus said so much with so little:

"Father, I thank You that You have heard Me. I knew that You always hear Me; but because of the people standing around I said it, so that they may believe that You sent Me."[6]

"Abba! Father! All things are possible for You; remove this cup from Me; yet not what I will, but what You will."[7]

"Father, forgive them; for they do not know what they are doing."[8]

"My God, my God, why have you forsaken me?"[9]

"Father, into your hands I commit my spirit."[10]

I was awestruck that such simple phrases would move God to act.[11]

And I found comfort in knowing that I'm not the only Jesus follower who stumbles forward in prayer. The disciples search for steady footing and approach their Rabbi asking him how best to pray. Jesus encourages them to resist flashy, monotonous prayers whose only purpose is to try to win God's favor, wear down God's resolve, or appear spiritual to others. Jesus introduces prayer as the acknowledgment that God, our Abba Father, already knows everything and waits for us to call on him. God sits enthroned, ready to listen, to help.

Jesus provides a specific prayer as a model. Rabbis of the day customarily gave their disciples prayers they could use habitually. Jesus' response to his disciples, known as the Lord's Prayer, is his most famous. The early church offered this prayer three times a day, following the ancient Jewish rhythm of prayer: morning, afternoon, and evening.

In the Lord's Prayer, I began to glimpse the wonder of prayer I experienced through Lent. The Son of God is asked how to pray, and he gives us fewer than five dozen words—an even shorter version appearing in the Gospel of Luke. Grocery lists run longer. The prayer can be spoken in a single breath, easily recited by children, jotted down in a few moments. Every. Word. Matters.

This brief prayer encompasses both the nearness of God in the present and the great hope of communion with God in the future. The Lord's Prayer is for today and also understood through the lens of eschatology, or end times. God's name is hallowed through the final destruction of his enemies and the salvation of his people. The imagery alludes to partaking of the bread at the messianic banquet and receiving forgiveness from God on judgment day. And we seek deliverance from the final judgment. The beauty of the Lord's Prayer is in its breadth and scope. Even if a googol of volumes are penned, they don't begin to scratch the surface of all Jesus communicated, the splendor displayed, the mysteries depicted.[12]

"Our *Abba* Father who is in heaven,

Hallowed be Your name.

Your kingdom come.

Your will be done,

On earth as it is in heaven.

Give us this day our daily bread.

And forgive us our debts, as we also have forgiven our debtors.

And do not lead us into temptation, but deliver us from evil."[13]

Renowned for its symmetry and simplicity, Jesus' prayer offers two sets of three petitions. The first three petitions focus on God—his divine nature, the coming of his kingdom, the fulfilling of his will. The second set of petitions shifts the attention toward us and includes humble requests for provision, forgiveness, protection. Though the prayer is personal in nature, the use of the word *our* reminds us that we are part of a vast kingdom, a community of believers who all need these things.

The prayer begins with God. Unlike any other rabbi of his time, Jesus calls his heavenly Father "Dad," or "Papa," or what is known in Aramaic as *Abba*. The name represents intimacy, affection, respect—invoking the image of a parent whose love cannot be measured, whose approval cannot be earned. We do not cry out to an unknown God; our petitions are not sent "To Whom It May Concern" but are addressed to a father who abounds in love.

Jesus' first petition is that God's name, which embodies his character, be hallowed or honored as holy. This isn't merely an acknowledgment of holiness but a call to holiness. More than a spiritual nod, the first words of the Lord's Prayer are a powerful petition:

Peel back the curtain. Reveal your holiness. Transform us forever.

The prayer reflects a renewed longing for God to make his name holy, not just in the heavens or in our world, but in our lives. Whenever we pray, *Hallowed be your name,* we're affirming the holiness of God, asking for a more intimate knowledge of God. Heads bow. Knees buckle. Calling on God's holiness exposes our impurity and displays his mercy.

The second and third petitions are simple but far from shallow. In asking that God's kingdom come, we're asking him to infiltrate every crevice of creation both now and in the future, in our hearts and in our world. God's kingdom is established in the now and the not yet, that which is near and that which is still far, far away. This robust prayer calls on God to extend his peace and justice and love and renewal everywhere for all time. Those who use this expansive prayer no longer walk with heads down, looking inward, because the prayer for God's kingdom challenges us to look all around for the abounding ways God answers.

The last set of petitions in the Lord's Prayer is brief but multifaceted as they remind us of our physical and spiritual dependence on God at all times. *Daily bread* draws on the imagery of the manna God provided the Israelites in the desert and was important for the people of Jesus' time who were hired on a daily basis. The petition for each day's bread addresses one of the most basic human fears: scarcity. Left unchecked, our fear of deprivation distorts the way we see ourselves, others, and God. Jesus' request for daily bread combats this fear with the loving reminder that all things come from God—and he wants to give us more than crumbs.

We are also reminded that forgiving and being forgiven are intimately intertwined. A healthy relationship with God requires us to maintain healthy relationships with each other. To experience uninhibited daily fellowship with God, we must choose to forgive. If we harbor accusations in our hearts toward others, we're not in a place to accept forgiveness from God. We cease to be a conduit of God's mercy and grace. Any lack of absolution for others reveals we may have lost sight of all that God has forgiven us.

Jesus concludes with the request that God lead us not into temptation but deliver us from evil. God never entices us with evil, but he does allow us to be tested and refined in our faithfulness. Sin will try to seduce us, challenging our fidelity and integrity. Though the presence of temptation in our lives is inescapable, through God's grace, strength, and provision, we do not have to succumb to any taunts. We can live ready to flee temptations of the flesh, of the world, and of the devil, finding deliverance from them all.

Such a prayer must have been shocking to pagans who

thought they would be heard because of their many words.[14] Jesus suggests something stark and uncomplicated in approach yet unfathomable in breadth. In a handful of brief stanzas, Jesus awakens holy desires to draw us closer to God. Such a concise prayer is a powerful reminder that, at times, I need to say less in order to pray more.

How often have I rattled on with God and said nothing at all? Relying on clichés, throwaway phrases, and high language I'd never use in everyday conversation, I took prayer for granted and lost sight of the wondrous opportunity to draw close to God.

How much are you really saying to God when you pray? Where has "nonversation" replaced conversation in your prayers? What slight shifts in your own prayer life could reignite your relationship with God?

We all need to become more intentional about prayer, selective about our words, ready to meet our Abba Father in the syllables and the silence that emerge. The wonder of prayer is rediscovered in *who* we're speaking to. Prayer is a mystical event by which we get to talk to the Creator of all—the One who fashioned our world with a few words—knowing that God not only listens but answers.

The months following Easter were marked by the temptation to forget Lent's lessons and return to my old ways. Time coaxed me to pack away my resurrection reflections and new-found prayer life. But I resisted and continue resisting because I've rediscovered the wonder of prayer—more majestic than I imagined. In those moments when I'm tempted to give in to my old ways, I recite the Lord's Prayer and return to the discipline of three-word prayers. Holding tight to these spiritual treasures, I now count down the days until Lent comes again.

.006:
TREASURE HUNTING
IN AFRICA

The Wonder of Restoration

STEPPING OUT OF THE AIRSTREAM TRAILER, I surveyed the office buildings filled with desks and computer screens. The energy of the city reverberated in the buzz of motorcycles, blaring car horns, and the barking of impatient taxi drivers. I took in a deep breath, imbibing the beauty of the skyline that is Cape Town, South Africa.

Most visitors opt for a familiar hotel chain, but Leif and I booked an off-the-beaten-path adventure at a "trailer park in the sky." The Grand Daddy Hotel, known for its innovative lodging options, hauled seven vintage trailers onto its downtown rooftop and invited the city's top interior designers to give them a splash of hipster. The stylists embellished each Airstream with its own theme, ranging from Elvis to the Wizard of Oz. We reserved Goldilocks and the Three Bears, a chrome trailer whose embellishments retold the classic fairy tale—complete with a bear suit and Goldilocks outfit, which were intriguing until we calculated how many previous guests might have used them.

Grabbing a bite at a downtown eatery, I noticed a wiry blonde woman with flyaway hair and electric blue eyes wearing a name tag from the same gathering we were attending.

"Let me guess: you're from Sweden or Norway," I said.

"Close!" she said. "Montana."

Sophia served as a professor of religious studies at a private university. As our conversation progressed, I appreciated Sophia's joyful disposition, quick wit, and keen observations on all we were experiencing. More than anything, though, I soon discovered I could be myself with her. Like two teenagers who met at camp and swapped stories while roasting marshmallows underneath a starry sky, Sophia and I became inseparable.

Often God places people in our paths who spark internal joy simply by being themselves. I found such a gift in Sophia. After a few days of bemoaning being trapped in a conference center, Sophia and I decided to spend an afternoon playing hooky and exploring the city together. We spent hours shopping in open-air markets, touring the Apartheid museum, and visiting various historical locations. Toward the end of the afternoon, she asked where else I wanted to visit.

My mind flashed back to the night we checked in at the Grand Daddy Hotel. The clerk handed me a tourist map with all Cape Town's attractions marked by colorful shapes. Scanning the street names, restaurants, and popular tourist destinations, a place denoted by a tiny red diamond had captured my imagination.

"Let's see the Jewel of Africa," I said.

"What is it?" she asked.

"The map doesn't say, but anything called the Jewel of Africa must be magical!" I assured her.

I estimated the journey required several miles of walking, but the hike promised a reward, I reasoned—after all, we were embarking on a grand adventure.

The ultimate portrait of a tourist, I held out my treasure map at the corner of a busy intersection, trying to navigate the best and safest path. Some of the narrower empty streets caused us to look over our shoulders and increase our pace. We stuck close together in this city renowned for its crime.

I learned more about Sophia's story as we wove through the streets. During graduate school, Erik, a fellow student, asked her out on a coffee date. She agreed to meet him under a tree in the center of the school courtyard but soon forgot. Erik extended grace for her no-show and continued pursuing her. The rescheduled coffee date blossomed into an entire day together where they shared common experiences and dreams for the future. Love's fingers grabbed their hearts and drew them together. One evening, Erik confessed he wanted to marry her. Sophia didn't hesitate. More than anything, she wanted to spend the rest of her life with Erik.

The couple began whiteboarding their futures together. Despite his many strengths, Erik had one permanent weakness. Born with a congenital heart defect, he had undergone surgery as a teenager to repair a missing flap on one of his valves. Doctors told him he'd require open-heart surgery later in his life but during an annual checkup discovered the surgery was needed sooner than anticipated.

Driving to the hospital for the surgery, neither Sophia nor Erik worried about the outcome. The doctors had explained that any threat to Erik's life or long-term health was less than 5 percent. The statistic was based on studies of patients who were often in poor physical health. Eric was young, athletic, in love.

The surgery was scheduled to last seven hours but required nearly twenty-one. Erik's family and Sophia waited for updates. Somewhere around hour fourteen, Erik's body stopped clotting blood. The doctors began administering pint after pint to keep Erik alive. When the surgery concluded, a machine kept Erik's heart beating. His body refused to respond to the withdrawal of anesthesia.

A series of tests revealed a loose brain clot had destroyed his mental capacity. Erik's major organs started shutting down. Two days after surgery, Erik died.

"I knew it was a possibility," Sophia said. "But I never owned it. I never thought I'd leave the hospital to help plan a funeral."

Sophia helped choose which friends delivered eulogies, served as pallbearers, and performed music at his funeral. She held every-thing together until the crowd left. Then she allowed herself to feel the Gothic tones of loss and grief. When Erik died, a piece of her died too.

In the wake of his death, the support Sophia received felt hollow—as if people delivered balloons with the helium already leaking out. Many of the well-meaning but trite responses of friends and those in her faith community were more damaging than healing.

Some suggested the heart malfunction was a gift from God. Others alluded to the idea that his death was a result of sin—in her life or her fiancé's. Still others questioned if she could ever date again. Almost as painful as the people who offered cruel comments were those who disappeared. Unsure of what to say or how to deal with the situation, some of her closest friends said nothing at all. Sophia found herself abandoned and iso-lated, wrestling with unanswerable questions.

But a professor at Sophia's university refused to give up on her.

"This professor never felt he needed to correct me but rather made the journey with me, providing time and space to come to grips with what my faith looked like on the other side of Erik's death," she told me.

The professor asked tough questions of Sophia and allowed her to ask tough questions back. Neither balked. They wrestled through ideas and emotions. At times, in the midst of confusion and apathy, he simply sat with her saying nothing at all. Months rolled by.

In fits and spurts, her faith developed a pulse. Sophia began to allow herself not only to feel but to come back to life again. Experiencing unconditional, radical compassion proved potent and transformative for Sophia. Love liberated her.

"Through Erik's death, I'm more comfortable not always knowing the answers," she said. "Though at the same time, I feel more confident in the core of what I believe and what I know to be true. The experience has informed the way I teach and allowed me to become gentler in how I do theology with others."

"Where are you in the process of becoming alive again?" I pressed.

"Struggling, like the butterfly," she said. "A cocoon is always dark and thick when you're on the inside."

"Do you still have questions for God?"

"Just a few million or so, but I did get one question answered."

"What's that?"

"The professor who reached out to me—the one who let me ask tough, ugly questions of life and God—well, I spoke to him awhile back and asked him why he didn't let go, why he didn't give up on me."

"What did he say?" I asked, hanging on her words.

"He said he saw life in me."

I stopped walking and lowered the map as her words hung suspended, thick, in the air. This professor, this chance acquaintance, saw life in Sophia and fought back hell to retrieve her. Others walked away; he refused to budge. Though hundreds of students filed through his classroom each semester, thousands roamed the halls of his prestigious school, he fought for one, this one, because in her he had seen life.

Listening to Sophia, I realized that when the registrar assigned her this particular professor at that time in her life it wasn't a coincidence. Among a wide selection of potential schools and possible professors, God had been actively at work orchestrating a wondrous masterpiece of divine restoration. Sophia was a living, breathing example of the wonder of restoration.

She revealed the faithfulness of God and his commitment to restore us—no matter what we've experienced. Like spiritual smelling salts, Sophia awoke me to the wonder that God is in the business of restoration. God is committed to bringing us to wholeness and transforming us into conduits of his redemption and renewal.

The professor recognized the spark of divine life in Sophia and through loving compassion rekindled her faith. *He* didn't restore Sophia. God did. But God often prefers not to work solo. Sophia's story alerted me to how often I pass by uncounted opportunities to participate in the restorative work of God. Asleep to the work of God all around, I fail to join in the marvelous event. How many people have I dismissed that I should have embraced? How many sparks of life have I extinguished rather than rekindled? How many times have I refused the invitation to join God in his supernatural work?

Like the Old Testament prophet Ezekiel, all I see are dry bones.

Counted among thousands of Jews exiled to Babylon, Ezekiel becomes a political and religious prisoner whom God selects as his mouthpiece. Ezekiel experiences a spate of divine visions, riddles, and parables that pulsate with rich imagery. He prophesies the toppling of Jerusalem, the judgment on nations who rejoice in its destruction, the hope of freedom for those trapped in captivity. Like his contemporaries, Ezekiel calls people to shut their ears to false prophets and abandon idolatry.[1]

One of the most startling scenes the prophet encounters is a valley full of skeletal remains.

Skulls and scapulas.

Vertebrae and ribs.

Femurs and phalanges.

Shoulder blades and tailbones.

Ezekiel makes the archaeological discovery of a lifetime.

"Can these bones live?" the Lord asks.[2]

Unsure how to respond to this potentially trick question, Ezekiel admits he has no idea: only God knows. God perhaps takes pleasure in this answer because he invites Ezekiel into the process of speaking life into a graveyard. As the syllables leave Ezekiel's lips, the prophet hears the soft clacking of cartilage as the bones click together. Ezekiel watches as tendons sprout and sew bones to flesh.

Again, the Lord tells Ezekiel to speak life to the boneyard. A miracle unfolds before his eyes: the same Spirit who breathes life in the beginning also breathes life in the end. The prophet feels the air sucked out of the scene as tens of thousands of lungs take in their first breath. Instead of a bone yard, the prophet stands before a sea of sparkling eyes and pink cheeks, life beaming in all directions. The wonder of restoration probably took Ezekiel's breath away.

The prophetic scene becomes a potent message of encouragement for the Jews, a promise of their return to Israel and restoration after captivity. Israel had been dispersed, splintered in a thousand irreconcilable pieces. God promises to bring them together again.

In reflecting on Ezekiel's imagery, I found myself fiddling with the question: *When I look at others, do I see dry bones or the children of God?* On more days than I want to admit, I find myself distracted by the lifelessness, instead of the possibilities. I lose sight of the truth that God's perspective is wildly different from mine. Ezekiel's vision not only serves as a challenge to love and serve and hope and wait but also to speak life. Ezekiel's encounter isn't just an ancient prophetic word but a reminder of what we've been entrusted with as children of God. To exhale life, the same God-life breathed in us, to others. Yet how often do we miss finding God in the graveyard?

How often do we mistake children of God for piles of bones?

Rather than become involved, we retreat, recoiling at the scene and scent of the carcasses. Yet the wondrous calling of God on our lives is to become conduits of a holy replenishment. As children of God, we're meant to live on high alert, watching for the possibility of divine restoration in the lives of those around us. We're called to look where no signs of life are found, where others dismiss its possibility. And we're invited to speak life—words of encouragement, hope, and peace that embody the goodness of God—whenever possible.

The wonder of restoration is exemplified through the visions of an exiled Old Testament prophet, and realized throughout the life of Christ. In Jesus' journeys, he routinely looked on piles of dead bones, people the religious leaders dismissed, and spoke life, leaving those who watched awestruck by the wonder of restoration. Such moments invite us to inhale and exhale divine restoration more fully.

One of the most meaningful encounters for me is the story of blind Bartimaeus—someone who never selects the hardships he experiences in this life; they're preselected for him. Can't most of us relate? Though God forbids mistreating the blind, the ancient world lacked effective treatment or support, leaving many to suffer in darkness without hope.[3] Shoved to the margins of society, Bartimaeus grew up uneducated and poor, dependent on begging as a means of survival.

Bartimaeus finds a place on a ribbon of road where he announces to bystanders, "Give to God!" as an initiation and challenge for everyone in earshot to demonstrate honor and compassion. Whenever a gift is received, Bartimaeus, like the other beggars, declares in loud voice the giver's nobility and asks for God's blessing. The public praise is a token of gratitude in exchange for the alms.[4]

Without physical vision, Bartimaeus develops a strong listening ear. When someone mentions that Jesus of Nazareth is among the crowd leaving the city, Bartimaeus sucks in extra oxygen before hollering, "Jesus, Son of David, have mercy on me!"[5] Bartimaeus acknowledges Jesus as the promised Messiah, King David's descendant for whom Israel has been waiting.

Onlookers try to drown out Bartimaeus' voice.

Be quiet.

Enough.

Hush.

They attempt to silence the rustling from the dry bones. But the opposition only makes Bartimaeus squawk louder. He's no fool. Bartimaeus knows those he annoys may pull their financial support in the future, but he's only concerned with one person in the entire crowd. Jesus stops in his tracks and instructs his disciples to call the blind man.

Bartimaeus throws off his coat, possibly his only possession, and hightails it to the Son of God. The blind man is greeted with one of the simplest yet startling questions, "What do you want Me to do for you?"[6]

For those studying the Gospel of Mark, the question is familiar. Fifteen verses earlier, Jesus asks the same of two of his closest disciples, James and John. The sons of Zebedee jockey for the highest position among Jesus' followers and ask for an extraordinary honor. Yet Bartimaeus desires something far more humble and ordinary. And Jesus meets him there—not as a problem or victim but as a person—just as he does us.

Like all the questions Jesus asks, he already knows the answer, but the inquiry provides a moment of honest self-reflection. Bartimaeus didn't choose blindness, but will he choose sightedness? Will he give up everything familiar to seize the unknown? Will he ask for restoration and the fullness of life to be breathed into his bones?

The man who only knows blindness chooses healing. Jesus speaks life: "Go, your faith has healed you."[7]

Bartimaeus' eyes open for the first time. Rubbing his face, he looks and finds colors flapping in the wind before they take shape. The colors grow brighter with each passing moment. Hues unimaginable. Pigments unexpected. Unlocked from the darkness, he sees beauty everywhere. Awestruck faces surround him in the wake of the miracle they've witnessed: a blind man fully restored.

But the wonder of restoration goes even deeper.

Woven into the fabric of this story is a detail that's easy to overlook: the mention and double meaning of Bartimaeus. With the exceptions of Jesus' friend Lazarus, who was raised from the dead, and Malchus, whose ear was cut off by Peter, Bartimaeus stands as the only healing miracle with a name. Everyone else is identified in less specific terms, such as the "demon-possessed man," the "cleansed leper," or the "afflicted woman."

In ancient culture, popular theology dictated that blindness was a sign of God's punishment for sin or defilement. Those familiar with the Aramaic translation of Bartimaeus (*t m '*) as "son of filth" or "son of defilement" understood his name to be consistent with his lot in life. But the Greek version of the name (*tim*) can be translated "son of honor." When Jesus heals Bartimaeus, he's in essence revealing who Bartimaeus is called and created to be all along. Jesus isn't just restoring his physical sight but his dignity as a child of God. The story opens with Bartimaeus sitting by the road and ends with him following Jesus on the road.[8]

Jesus' gift to Bartimaeus is free but not without cost. Bartimaeus needs to give up all that is familiar to grasp what Christ has for him. Bartimaeus acknowledges his blindness but refuses to allow it to hold him back. Though the crowd tells him to hush, Bartimaeus chooses to take responsibility for his faith and his future. He doesn't worry about what others think, only God. In the process, Bartimaeus receives the new life God intends.

When it comes to the restoration business, Jesus owns the entire franchise. The Son of God spends his days reaching the marginalized, healing the smashedhearted, setting people free from torment, and raising corpses back to life. Everywhere Jesus travels, he affirms life and welcomes people into a restored relationship with God and each other. And he coaches his disciples to carry on the same ministry. When Jesus sends out the twelve, he essentially tells them to find dry bones and breathe life into them. He instructs, "Heal the sick, raise the dead, cleanse the lepers, cast out demons. Freely you received, freely give."[9] Jesus makes his disciples conduits of the restorative work of God.

Reflecting on the stories of Ezekiel and Bartimaeus renews my desire to recognize life where at first I saw only death, to see divine possibilities where at first I saw only impossibilities, to join God in the wondrous work of restoration he's doing in lives everywhere.

Dodging traffic at every turn, I hunted treasure alongside someone who was once a pile of bones. I marveled as Sophia bounded across noisy streets with laughter, vibrant with life, radiating God's love. In her previous condition, would I have passed by or taken pause to become involved? Would I have recognized the spark of life or only the sting of death? Would I have fought with the same compassionate tenacity as the professor?

I can't say for sure. But Sophia's presence reawakens me to

the wonder that God places life inside each of us and invites us to recognize this life in each other. Breathing restoration is one of the most powerful displays of God's unflinching love. As we breathe God's restoration into our own lives, we are better able to exhale his restoration to others. When we breathe out restoration, we spread the goodness of God. When we breathe out restoration, we release grace and hope immeasurable. When we breathe out restoration, we join God as he beats back hell and unleashes heaven on behalf of those he's created. More than any other person I encountered in South Africa, Sophia made me want to breathe in and out the fullness of divine restoration.

Will you be a person who sees life in mere bones? Will you believe and respond to those who are on the side of the road? Will you be someone who breathes life into others?

Breathing life begins with the simplest of actions. See someone. Really see. As you reach out and interact, offer your full attention to whoever is in front of you. Listen to someone. Really listen. Give someone the gift of your presence—your fully present, undivided attention. Pray for someone. Really pray. Though it may feel awkward in the moment, ask if you can offer a prayer, and bless the person with kindness. Give to someone. Really give of yourself. Find an unexpected way to help someone whose needs remain unmet. Radiate the generosity of Christ.

Standing before a metal address plate, I double-checked the map. I was surprised the Jewel of Africa lacked noticeable signage but hoped we'd still be rewarded for our hard-fought expedition. A receptionist and security guard sat inside the narrow entrance to the building.

"We're here to see the Jewel of Africa," I announced.

"You've come to the right place," the receptionist replied. "How did you hear about us?"

"The map from the hotel," I explained. "We followed the red diamond. But I'm still not sure—what is the Jewel of Africa?"

"You'll see!" the security guard said. "Just sign in here."

Sophia and I provided our names and addresses then followed the guard up a narrow stairway and through a locked door.

"This is the Jewel of Africa!" he said.

The room opened to rows of jewelry cases and shelves of sculptures, artwork, saltshakers, and T-shirts. The Jewel of Africa was a tourist shop. Our chests sank, and we stared at each other in silence.

How often do we encounter these seeming disappointments in life? Searching for an unfamiliar treasure that might be around the next corner, we miss out on the relationships, opportunities, and challenges God has placed in our midst.

Sophia and I both realized the journey together had still been valuable. We decided to celebrate our epic discovery by purchasing a few items to take home, but for me, one of the great jewels of my time in Africa was hearing details of Sophia's story and how God breathed restoration in her through a kind professor. Sophia reminded me that no matter what *I* see, God sees life. The same life he breathes giving my soul a shape, my spirit a redeemed nature. Now I want to live with eyes wide open to the treasures around me so I can breathe anew in others.

To this day, we still chuckle about our adventure together. We later learned that the real Jewel of Africa isn't any particular stone but an affectionate name for Cape Town, the city whose streets we'd explored. Without realizing, we'd been relishing the treasure all day.

.007:
THE MAGIC
IN THE TABLE

The Wonder of Friendship

TWO AND A HALF YEARS AFTER our move to Juneau, Alaska, the time came for another transition—this time to Colorado. Having moved many times in my life, I find the process of uprooting both challenging and invigorating.

Living among stacks of crates, packing tape, and bubble wrap reminds me that being unsettled isn't just an emotion. In the process of boxing photos and knickknacks, I tend to cruise down memory lane to relationships and events of years past. After weeks of sorting, compiling, and discarding, there's always an interlude that I long for but somehow least expect, when I walk back into our home only to discover emptiness. Though baseboards still need to be wiped down and bathrooms cleaned, an eerie silence fills the place as the present shifts to the past— the home where we live becomes the home where we lived.

Then comes the moment I look forward to the most. After

handing the keys over to the landlord or new owner, I climb into the car and drive away. Any sense of sadness or loss is momentarily replaced by the exhilaration of endless possibilities. I feel wildly free. After an hour or so, the elation subsides, and I succumb to a new reality: I'm starting over again.

I felt all these emotions as we transitioned to Colorado. After months of scouring real estate websites, we found a two-story home on the outskirts of a tiny town known as Morrison, on the edge of Colorado's Rocky Mountains. The inside needed some updating, but the back porch opened to a breathtaking view of the mountains with the Denver skyline in the distance. The home sat securely outside our price range, but the real estate agent encouraged us to make a bid anyway. To our surprise, the offer was accepted.

The owner explained she was a follower of Jesus as we signed the final closing paperwork. At our first showing, by chance, she had been home. She told us that when she saw us walk through the door, she knew we were supposed to live at this address—a place she cherished. She reached across the closing table, grabbed my hand, looked into my eyes, and assured me we were meant to live in this home. Her words delivered divine delight.

Our furniture unpacked, our clothes tucked away, I knew the time had come to start building a new life. We began in our neighborhood. When a couple strolled past our driveway, we rushed out to greet them. As we worked in the yard, we waved and said hello to anyone who came out to retrieve their mail.

But the "Hey, neighbor" conversations never moved beyond anything surfacy and shallow.

The isolation intensified with Christmas. Aloneness became loneliness. I needed to become more proactive. Inspired by the holidays, I decided to spend a day baking one of my childhood favorites—challah. I kneaded and braided each loaf of lightly sweetened bread, traditionally eaten by Jews on the Sabbath, with loving care. I delivered a hot loaf to more than a dozen neighbors with a handwritten card, tossing in a bottle of red wine for good measure. I made sure to say a few kind words then left before I wore out my welcome. Though I doubt they ever knew, I wanted to greet my neighbors by blessing them and serving them a kind of communion.

When we returned home, I waited for responses like a schoolchild eager for the recess bell. A few days later, Leif discovered a single thank-you note on our front doorstep taped to a plastic plate of holiday cookies.

We shared even fewer conversations with our neighbors once winter blanketed everything with snow. After the New Year, I resolved to invite some acquaintances from church into our home for a meal. Serving grilled steak fajitas with fresh guacamole and homemade pico de gallo, we shared our story and listened to theirs. The evening came to a close with the promise of getting together soon, but we never heard from them again.

We reached out to several others from the church and neighborhood, even mixing up the menu to see if different types of food helped people connect. The initial conversation around our dining room table required effort but improved as the meal progressed. By the time our guests left, I was hopeful we had made new friends, but none of our invitations were reciprocated.

I began to think Leif and I were less interesting than I thought we were. Or maybe we smelled skunky. Despite doing everything I knew to initiate relationships—inviting people into our home, serving them a fresh homemade meal, steering clear of any divisive topics, even gathering around a circular dining room table, which is supposed to be the best design for connection—we remained friendless.

Yet I refused to give up. *Making friends always takes time*, I assured myself. Deciding to give it another whirl, we welcomed Mark and Leslie, acquaintances from work, into our home. When they arrived, we scrambled to finish cooking the barbecued chicken. They didn't seem to mind and joined us in the kitchen to chat as we sliced, diced, and scooped food into serving dishes.

"We're ready!" I announced.

"What about the table?" Leif asked.

In our harried preparation, I had forgotten to set the formal dining room table.

"Let's grab plates, dish up the food buffet style, and gather around the old table in the living room," Leif suggested on a whim.

I shrugged, figuring nothing could lower our current track record. Mark and Leslie filled their plates and nestled into the leather couch. Leif plopped into his favorite chair. I sat cross-legged on the living room floor next to the old coffee table. That's when the magic happened.

Conversation danced like the vivid warm flames of our fireplace. Topics shifted from work and play to theology and technology. We exchanged honest stories of heartaches and celebration. We laughed hard and often. The connection I craved in friendship was satisfied. More than anything I didn't want the evening to end. I experienced the wonder of friendship, and I never wanted to let go.

Lying in bed after all we experienced, I reflected on what made that night together so special. I dismissed the food as an option. The sugary barbecue sauce burned one side of the chicken. The potatoes turned out too firm. Remembering stories about their close friends and family, I ruled out that our guests were lonely. What could it be?

Maybe the magic lay in the table.

The rustic tabletop that anchors our living room is an antique barn door made of hand-carved mesquite and marred by years of heavy use. One of the corners of the table boasts rusty barbed wire used to hold the frame together; another is rounded where the door used to hinge. The table's surface is wildly uneven, scarred by knots and holes. If you're not careful you can easily tip a glass on one of the four railroad spikes that connect the four-inch-thick wooden slab to its base—a rustic yoke for oxen. The table receives support from two sets of bowed pieces of wood acting as legs. In one of the narrow pockets where the wood is hemmed together rests the remnants of previous owners, including an assortment of crumbs, a dried leaf, and a red poker chip I've never been able to extract.

I adored our living room table from the moment we purchased it. Having sold most of our furniture before leaving Alaska, the hunt for comfy couches and contemporary lighting began as soon as we arrived in Colorado. I spent most of my time looking for one-of-a-kind pieces on Craigslist and sorted through hundreds of ads each day looking for the treasures that would transform our house into a home.

One day I stumbled on a post for a brand-new California king-size mattress. I dialed the number and arranged for a time later that morning to connect, assuring Leif the drive would be well worth the effort. Unfamiliar with the area, I was surprised when the address led us to an expansive mountain getaway overlooking the valleys below. Walking up the stone stairs to the front door, I tugged on Leif's sleeve, "We should ask if they're selling anything else."

"It's just the mattress, honey," he said.

"We should still ask," I persisted.

When I posed the question to the grey-haired, middle-aged businessman who greeted us at the door, he pointed his fingers upward, looked in both directions, and declared, "Everything's for sale!" Then he handed me a price list.

As an executive of a large telecommunications firm, he had been transferred to Los Angeles, where his wife was already purchasing furniture for their new glass house. In awe, we walked through room after room, handpicking everything we needed—from the brick-red bench now resting in our entryway to the armoire in our living room that looks like stacked luggage. But of all the pieces we purchased, I most prize the old, thick table we gathered around with Mark and Leslie.

The morning after our new friends joined us for dinner, I called Leif into the living room.

"There's magic in the table," I said, thumping the wooden frame with confidence.

"Maybe last night was a fluke," Leif said with a skeptical eye. "Let's invite more people over and try again."

A few nights later we hosted Andy and April for dinner. When the time came to eat, we conveniently "forgot" to set the dining room table again and gathered in the living room instead. Once more the conversation brimmed—chockablock with life and laughter and authenticity. We felt the warmth of human companionship and delighted in the work God was doing in all of our lives. When we said goodnight at the end of the evening, we had a hunch we'd made some lifelong friends.

After the dishes were dried, I sat on the couch in the living room, inspecting the table. *Maybe it's the table. It can't be the table,* I reasoned. *There's no magic in the table. There's absolutely no magic in this table.*

Wait a minute! My mouth cracked open. I traced the last ten months in my mind. From waving to neighbors across the street to bolting out of their driveways after dropping off a loaf of bread to trite conversations in stiff settings, we had kept others at arm's length. Up until that point, I knew *what* we were missing but not *why* we were missing it. I embraced the shallowness of a hundred "Hey, neighbor" conversations without ever letting my guard down. Even when I delivered challah bread, I never entered anyone's home. The encounters were brief, limited, safe. Though I beckoned people with one hand to come closer, I extended the other palm out holding them back. Instead of creating appropriate boundaries with people that allowed for healthy, life-giving exchanges—as my counselor recommended—I built walls that kept people out.

In our living room, however, I risked vulnerability. This room is the space where I take naps, snuggle with my husband, cry after a bad day. In the kitchen, I'm "Margaret, the affable host," but in the living room, I'm just Margaret. Just me.

To rediscover the wonder of friendship, I had to change. Rather than holding people back, I needed to invite them in. My hands required unclenching and my soul exposing. I had to learn to be more freely myself—more focused on the rewards of good relationship than the possibility of being hurt. When we gathered around the table in our living room, my heart laid out a welcome mat.

The temptation to live a guarded life allures everyone, but walls constructed for protection ultimately lead to isolation. When we develop healthy boundaries and a sustainable rhythm in life, we have more—not less—time for deep, meaningful relationships.

Receiving the life God has for you requires vulnerability. God wants you to build a life without walls—one in which he is your protection—allowing you to live with arms wide open, where you can know and be fully known. Such a place doesn't exist without moments of hurt, rejection, and misunderstanding, but in this posture, you lay hold of the wonder of friendship God intended all along.

Though our living room table isn't magical, as I sit on the couch, feet perched on its wooden frame, and review its scars, I recognize the antique as symbolic of the wonder God had been awakening in my life. The table is physically composed of rich and meaningful imagery, its surface an actual door—representative of opportunity and invitation, hope and possibility.

Doors line our lives. Glance down the hallway of an apartment complex or a suburban street, and doors align in every direction. Some wait to be opened; others remain shut no matter how long fists beat against their frames. Much of life is spent selecting which doors to knock on, enter, and exit, and much of our time around our table is spent discussing those choices.

Doors are not the same as a room. We don't live in doorways; we pass through them. That may be one reason Jesus drew on this rich symbol in his teachings—he knew the temporary nature of this earthly life all too well. *I am the door. I stand at the door. Choose the narrow door.* Jesus himself passed through the doorway of two worlds when he donned the uniform of human flesh. He used the imagery of a door, maybe one as heavy and worn as our tabletop, to beckon people to communion with God.[1] Through Christ, we can be ushered from the mundane and predictable to a whole new life and world.

When I reflect on my journey with God, I realize I've passed by a thousand doors in the form of opportunities but only entered a few. Glancing back over my shoulder to doors of opportunity I've passed, some marked by many prayers and others by far too few, I find myself second-guessing what would have happened if I had passed through.

I know that many doors are far better left closed. God warns Cain that sin crouches at the door, but Cain chooses to turn the knob, allowing the tensions of jealousy and anger to overwhelm him, and walks straight through. He kills his brother and passes over a threshold of no return.[2]

Other doors testify to God's safety. Protection. Grace. Like the door slamming behind Noah and his family after they are safely on the ark, or the door protecting Lot and his loved ones from being kidnapped.[3] To the spiritually tepid, like those at the church of Laodicea, Jesus announces he's standing at the entry-way knocking. He refuses to kick down the frame and barge in. Instead, he waits—patient but persistent—for an invitation, standing ready with the spiritual nourishment our spirits crave.[4]

On the night of his arrest, Jesus tells his followers that he is no longer calling them servants because those in the service of a master don't have an idea what the one they serve is thinking or planning. Jesus renames his disciples "friends"—because he shares everything he hears from the Father.[5]

Now, the title of being the "Lord's servant" was already one of honor. Only a handful of people were given this privileged title throughout the Old Testament—including Moses, David, and Isaiah. Abraham alone received the titles of both servant and friend.[6]

When Jesus calls his followers "friends," he isn't just speaking to those in the Upper Room before his death but to his disciples for generations to come. I find myself awestruck every time I consider that the Creator of the universe not only calls me friend but desires to walk in greater intimacy and affection with me each and every day.

God longs for both intimate friendship one-on-one and for us to discover friendship within a community. Yet experiencing the wonder of friendship with others requires us to let our guard down and allow others to pass through the doors not only of our homes but our lives.

I love the reflections and insights inspired by that rugged

old door-turned-tabletop. But the second part of the table offers lessons as well: the yoke.

The base is a yoke. I never dreamed of having a wooden yoke for oxen sitting in the middle of my living room. But this curvy piece provides the support for the heavy barn door table-top. The frame also reminds me of the Scripture. In one of his most beloved discourses, the Son of God turns to those who are overworked and heavy-laden with the burdens of the religious leaders' legalities and regulations and exhorts them to come, take his yoke.[7]

The wonder of the invitation is that Jesus isn't asking us to be his farm animal but his friend as our yoke mate. Jesus' call isn't to independence but interdependence—to plow, to pull together for the long haul. Through the mystery of Christ, a tool of oppression is transformed into a cloak of freedom.[8]

When the old barn door and wooden yoke were fastened together, they formed a table—a symbol of connection, a holy relic of sorts. This is the rustic, battered-around-the-edges place we now gather for meals. The process of eating together reveals our humanness, pulling back the façade of our self-sufficiency. In the simplicity of asking someone to pass the butternut squash, we're reminded we don't just need food but each other. We cannot go it alone.

Gathered around a table, we fill our bellies and our souls. We feast as we taste and see the Lord's goodness in our lives. The mystery of the table is that with mere wooden planks, a holy intersection emerges where ideas roll, tumble, and somersault between souls. Together, we learn to speak the unspeakables and discover grace. In this place, we share the delight of renewed hope and opportunities as well as our burdens and responsibilities, even the ache of stillborn dreams. We listen to truths that are sometimes painful to hear. In such tender moments of fellowship and friendship, we sense the sweet presence of God in our midst.

Such relationships and moments of friendship don't happen overnight. They take years to nurture and develop, but the rewards prove it is so worth the hard work. Over more afternoons and evenings than I can count since we've learned to let down our guard, I've sat before this table in awe of the wonder of relationship from which conversation flows.

Words are a gift through which we keep the past alive, the present bearable, the future hopeful. At this table I've encountered the mysteries of God, hearty questions of faith, breathtaking confessions of doubt. I've been reaffirmed that in the darkness of difficulties I face, I'm not alone—not the only one—and sometimes this simple knowledge gives me the courage to take the next step.

At this table I've seen a wellspring of tears unlocked, sometimes my own, and laughed until my belly ached. I've offered acceptance and received acceptance, being reminded that sometimes even the smallest changes are impossible without someone encouraging, "You are loved as you are." Afterward,

I've tucked myself into bed marveling at the mysterious healing that took place.

But not every evening ends so well. Sometimes portions of the meal are undercooked, the flavors don't come together, the conversation doesn't connect. Ideas and tidbits of news bat back and forth without any spark of real intimacy or interest. What surprises me most is that our evenings around the table—whether they leave me awestruck or yawning—can be shared by the same people. Much like life, one night proves unforgettable while the next begs to be forgotten. Yet we continue to come together, offering our unguarded selves, because we recognize every table as a place where humanity can gather.

Without effort, the table testifies to the beauty of imperfection. Full of character, the weathered, dilapidated surface is part of what makes the table great. The wavy lines in the wood are blotched from far too many spills collected over time. Around this table we've learned to celebrate our flaws, finding hidden beauty in our faults and in our frailty.

When we purchased this old-door-turned-table, we never dreamed of the entryway it would become in our lives or the lives of others. Make no mistake, there's nothing magical about the table; but when we gather around it we do so with the expectation that we'll share our hopes, our dreams, our lives with others as they share themselves with us.

Around this table, we forge new friendships and strengthen old.

Around this table, we mourn life's savage losses.

Around this table, we share syllables—the most unsuspecting of which become transformative.

Around this table, we laugh, we cry, we remember.

Around this table, maybe more than any other place, we live.

When I'm at home, somewhere around this table is where you'll find me most days. This table is where I share myself with God and others through a battered laptop, a place where I wrestle my fears to the ground in order to be known in the fullness of my humanity. This is the place I keep vigil on the deepest truths of my identity, a place where healing and hope are exchanged among longtime and soon-to-be friends.

We all need a table, a place where we gather to be fully and truly ourselves. Without such a place, we may lose track of our souls, embracing a cheap, snap-together fiberboard image of ourselves instead of the uneven, rustic, knotty reality that, when unveiled, reveals the mystery and beauty of the *imago dei*—the image of God. We need a place where we pray for a replenished wonder of friendship and wait for God to answer in unexpected ways.

When are you most tempted to hold people back at arm's length? When do you allow the temptation of living a guarded life to get the best of you? What are you doing to grow and nurture the meaningful relationships God has for you?

If you want to seize the wonder of friendship in your life, find your table. Discover that place—whether it's in your dining room or living room or favorite restaurant or coffee shop—where you can be fully yourself and warm your soul in the glow of both knowing and being known. And when you find this space, live with vulnerability. Pass freely through the doorway of friendship and bring along as many people as you can. Share your burdens, and give others a hand. Rediscover the lost art of conversation. Treasure the hidden wealth of comradeship. Know others from the inside out instead of merely the outside in.

When Leif and I waved good-bye to Alaska and said hello to Colorado, the uncertainty of our future both worried and energized us. Despite our quiet apprehension about the transition, we knew an adventure awaited. But we had no idea that the greatest exploits would unfurl inside our own home. Eating off our laps. Opening our lives to others. Gathering around a well-worn hunk of wood.

That table may not be magical, but it's sure seen some miracles.

.008
THE DISAPPEARING
SILVER NECKLACE

The Wonder of Forgiveness

THE NAME "EUGENE DAVIDSON" flashed across my computer screen, and for the first time in more than a year I felt nothing. Not a ripple of anger or animosity. No resentment or rage. Not even the slightest annoyance. In that moment, I realized I was finally free.

The journey was more difficult than I ever imagined.

More than a year before, I had received an unexpected call from our accountant telling me our payroll company, owned by Eugene Davidson, had failed to file and pay our taxes for much of the previous year. Through hundreds of hours of phone calls, we pieced together the details of a story that circled one painful truth: we had been embezzled.

The frustration was compounded by the knowledge that we had done our homework. Leif spent weeks researching payroll companies around the United States before selecting one that earned rave reviews online as well as a gold star Better Business Bureau rating. The company handled the payroll for major companies around the United States, and the owner ranked as one of the top business leaders in his state. We hired the company to withdraw money from our business account, issue checks to employees, and pay taxes due to the Internal Revenue Service each month.

Everything ran smoothly for more than a year until we received a notice that we'd missed a payment to the IRS. Alerting the payroll company to the error, we noticed the issue was fixed immediately. We never had another problem—until a series of notices from the IRS arrived.

That's when we discovered that while the company had filled out monthly paperwork for the IRS and withdrawn the funds for taxes, it never *actually* submitted the forms or paid the taxes. Instead, the company pocketed the funds. Phone calls and letters went unreturned. The company declared bankruptcy. Some estimates suggest the company conned more than eight hundred companies for upwards of twenty million dollars. When I spoke to a Secret Service agent about the issue, he told me, off the record, that with the amount of embezzlement taking place in our nation, this case wasn't worth their time. I refused to believe him.

Over the next few months, I spoke with anyone and everyone I could reach—the office of the state attorney general, the police detectives working on the case, the Secret Service, the

IRS, our accountant, and others. Like a battleship in a narrow canal, the search for answers filled in every gap in my life. I joined online discussion boards with others who had been duped—many of whom had been embezzled for much more— in order to understand the complexities of the case. Following websites for news updates became a daily chore. I couldn't look at Eugene Davidson's name or photo without wincing. Infuriated and outraged by the thievery of the owner of the company, a steely hatred hardened in my heart.

An unprecedented cry for justice howled within me. In our culture, *justice* is a buzzword, something we're to fight for on behalf of someone else, but all too often justice remains tenebrous and ambiguous. We know we want justice, but once it's in our grasp, we discover justice neither looks nor feels quite like what we expected. Through the embezzlement, the term became personal. I shrieked for justice—overwhelmed by a sea of information and infrastructure I didn't have the skills or know-how to navigate. I appealed to the IRS, which refused to forgive the debt. We paid all of our taxes a second time, this time making sure the money actually went to the government and not to an embezzler. Our request to waive the interest and penalties seemed fair, even just, but was denied nonetheless.

I felt like I'd been violated, as if someone smashed in one of our windows, climbed through, emptied my jewelry box, and left with all our valuables. Yet no one pursued the criminal. The cry for justice not only reverberated within us but with hundreds of other individuals and businesses who were also swindled. Current loopholes, or lootholes, in the law allow anyone to open a payroll company, giving them access to pilfer bank accounts. Without further regulation the abuses will continue; in fact, some of the executives involved in our payroll company have already started another.

The fraud left me distrustful. My psyche became hyperattentive to anyone who broke the most innocent of promises. I second-guessed the smallest inconsistencies and found myself living on high alert for anyone who hinted of being a shyster.

The embezzlement also upped the ante for a new temptation in my life. One day, I stopped by a department store to pick up a blouse. Browsing the racks, I glanced across the jewelry counter. Like a magpie magnetized by a shiny bottle cap, a stunning silver necklace mesmerized me. The delicate loops of the chain rolled between my fingers. The elegance of the simple design was remarkable. An unfamiliar urge overwhelmed me. More than anything, I wanted to slip the silver necklace into my jacket pocket and disappear out the door without paying. For a brief moment, I fantasized about the ease of the take. After all, the chain didn't have a security tag and the salespeople looked distracted. I scanned the walls and ceiling for security cameras— the only lens focused on the store entrance.

I snapped to my senses. *What was I thinking?*

I dropped the silver chain and barreled out of the store. On the drive home, I probed the depraved desire. Why did I want *that* necklace in *that* moment more than anything?

Temptation wasn't a stranger to me. In the past, temptation had crept into my life, urging me to take a second look at a sexy image; enjoy a second helping of dessert; tell the truth, just not the *whole* truth. The allure came in many guises—sexual sin, gluttony, lying; but stealing rarely, if ever, made an appearance. Over the next few weeks, however, temptation's persistence made me speculate if I was going to become a kleptomaniac.

In every store, I scanned the perimeter for security cameras. Waiting in line at a coffee shop, I estimated the time required to slip a mermaid-emblazoned mug into my purse. Filling my car with gas, I calculated the speed required to escape without paying. At a boutique, I needed to pry the boots off to prevent myself from walking out the door with a new pair. The primal urge to shoplift surged in my veins.

I prayed for the strength to resist the seduction of stealing and struggled to make sense of my life. One day I read a story of a woman who had been sold into modern-day slavery. She spent years of her life performing sexual acts at the commands of her captors. The police finally freed her. With the help of a nonprofit organization, she secured an education and started a business.

She rebuilt her life. But in the aftermath of the abuse, she confessed that it took every fiber in her mangled being to resist the seduction of mistreating others.

Reading her story helped me understand the temptations I faced. Having been abused, she felt the pull to abuse others. I had been defrauded, and now more than anything I wanted to steal from someone, anyone.

In the mire of my brokenness, I knew I needed to forgive Eugene Davidson, but the thought made me woozy. This man had violated our trust. His thievery had cost us wads of money, countless hours, immeasurable stress; the ordeal took a heavy emotional toll. The crimes testified to me that Davidson didn't deserve an acquittal. I reviewed Scripture passages that reminded me I wasn't the only one who felt this way.

In the Gospel of Matthew, Peter approaches Jesus about the practice of forgiveness. His question isn't whether or not to forgive but how many times to extend absolution. What motivated Peter to ask—a fresh perspective on a popular theological discussion or something far more personal? Maybe Peter wrestled with forgiveness in his life.

Scripture doesn't tell us the specifics of Peter's struggle or identify who mistreated him. I suspect the person behind Peter's question was a repeat offender—and possibly Peter had encountered more than one.

Throughout the Gospels, snapshots appear of Peter's competitive nature. When a debate emerges about which follower of Jesus is the greatest, Peter joins James and John in the battle for the grandiose title. When Mary Magdalene delivers the news of Jesus' death, Peter races a fellow disciple to the tomb only to fall behind, muscles blaring, lungs wheezing. And when Jesus reappears on the shore after the resurrection, Peter cannonballs into the water and swims to shore, reaching Jesus before any of the other disciples. Jockeying for position has a way of leaving everyone feeling manhandled. Though Peter often instigated the roughhousing, he probably felt battered from the tussles among the disciples. Maybe that contributed to his question.

Contemporary rabbis of Jesus' time sometimes limited absolution to three instances of premeditated sin, recognizing that any additional requests were probably not genuine. Peter probably suspects Jesus will be far more generous. Calculating three times isn't enough. Peter doubles the total, throws in an extra, and approaches Jesus.

The other disciples eavesdrop on Peter's question: "Lord, how often shall my brother sin against me and I forgive him? Up to seven times?"[1] For a brief moment, I imagine the disciples admiring the audacity of Peter's question and the apparent piousness of his suggested answer. Seven isn't only generous but also representative of the idea of completeness initiated during the seven days of creation.

But Peter's math is off. Though forgiving seven times may seem generous to rabbis, the number is only a fraction of what's required. When it comes to pardoning sins, Jesus calls us to exponential living. How many times is forgiveness required? Seventy times seven—more than anyone feels like offering and more than anyone wants to track. Jesus gave his disciples more than just a number, but a new way of life.

In essence, Jesus says, "Forgive wholly, and you will find yourself whole; forgive completely, and you will find yourself complete." Jesus goes on to tell a potent parable of two slaves. Drowning in debt, the king calls the first slave to repay everything he owes. Jesus never tells us the source of the slave's indebtedness—whether he overleveraged in a booming real estate market or harbored a secret gambling addiction. Regardless of how the slave amassed the debt, he owed the king ten thousand talents, a sum estimated in today's terms as nearly ten million dollars and much more in potential buying power in that day. Reflecting on this absurd amount for a slave to owe, some scholars believe Jesus relies on hyperbole to emphasize the impossibility of repayment.

When the slave confesses his inability to repay the debt, the king orders that he and his family be sold for repayment. The servant falls down and begs for patience, promising he'll repay everything. The king feels compassion and not only releases the slave but forgives the exorbitant debt, displaying a hardy grace.

Unfortunately, the slave suffers from short-term memory loss. He finds a fellow slave who owes him a single day's wages. Violently choking the fellow slave, he demands the small debt be repaid. The fellow slave begs for patience, promising repayment, but the forgiven slave refuses and throws his comrade in prison. When the king catches whiff of the injustice, he exposes the forgiven slave's lack of mercy and hands him over to the bouncers until everything is paid. The parable illustrates divine arithmetic, reminding us that whatever we forgive is chump change compared to how much we've been forgiven by God.

Reflecting on Jesus' response to Peter, I realized I'd become indifferent to the wonder of forgiveness and the incalculable debts God had forgiven me. My failure to forgive signaled that I had let go of the priceless treasure of God in my life. I had lost sight of the God who paints unspeakable beauty in the sky for people who neither deserve nor appreciate his work. I needed to be wonderstruck by forgiveness and grasp the grace of God again.

The wonder of forgiveness invites us to live alert to the work of God among us. All too often, a pardon follows an apology, an expression of sorrow, an act of repentance, or after a set of criteria has been met. But the absolution Jesus suggests to Peter is absurd. Jesus suggests that even when the apology becomes insincere, even when the person doesn't really mean what they're saying, even when you're beyond hope the other person will ever change, keep on dispensing grace. Jesus teaches Peter to embrace an inexhaustible forgiveness—one whose only condition is that we keep extending it.

My first efforts to forgive Eugene felt forced as I choked out a few words of absolution. I eventually reached a place where I could say, "I forgive you," aloud without hesitance, but the words on my lips didn't match what I still harbored in my heart. For a brief period, I thought changing up the way I said, "I forgive you," might help. I altered the pace and even emphasized the different syllables.

One morning I scribbled a prayer of amnesty, hoping something about placing pen on paper would make the forgiveness feel more real. The words flowed from my pen but not from my heart. Frustrated and angry, I confessed to God I didn't have the grace or strength to forgive and asked him to supply both in greater measure. Over the upcoming weeks he answered my prayer, and I found the words more heartfelt and sincere.

Along the way I discovered a facet of faith I never noticed before, the truth that forgiveness is not an action as much as a discipline. A solo acknowledgment of absolution or single act of disentanglement from the situation wasn't enough. I had to choose to forgive as though I were engaging in a spiritual discipline. Choosing to let go wasn't a one-time action but a required repetition month after month. Though I mentally chose to forgive, pouty emotions still surfaced with every notice from the IRS, every call from the accountant, and every breaking story of someone else being swindled by yet another crook.

Maybe this is one reason Jesus told Peter to forgive seven times seventy; he knew how many times total forgiveness sometimes takes. For me, somewhere between 372 and 379, I finally lost count and began to let go in the deeper recesses of my heart.

A very tough moment arrived when a group of individuals

embezzled by the payroll company organized a lawsuit against the head of the company. I was invited to join in. I felt torn. I craved justice and retribution but also recognized signing on meant an even greater level of involvement in the case for years to come. More than justice, more than the money, more than anything, I pined for freedom.

The decision over whether or not to become involved in a lawsuit became a watershed moment. When I mailed the notice that our company wasn't going to join, I crossed the threshold from captivity to liberation. Bitterness faded. Anger fled. Exhaling a sigh of relief, my muscles relaxed as though I'd just climbed off a massage table where all the knots in my neck and shoulders had been worked out. Until that moment, I'd been unaware of the anxiety I'd been harboring for months.

When others hurt us, the wounds they leave behind are sometimes gaping, leaving us breathless in the aftermath; or sometimes the wounds are shallow, and we don't realize the harm done until months later. However, when we don't allow the healing power of forgiveness to mend our injuries, we give opportunity for the infection of bitterness to ulcerate. A tiny scratch riddled with bacteria can become a candidate for amputation with enough time. Even the smallest of annoyances, when left unforgiven, can mutate into sources of great pain.

I was so consumed by the hurt and the injustice done to me, I hadn't noticed my ardor for God slowly slipping away. When I gave permission for enmity to fester, the fervor for

God cooled in my life. But the moment I slid the notice into the mailbox, I recognized the extent of how much I had been enslaved by unforgiveness and how much my lack of forgiveness had numbed my desire for God.

In choosing to forgive, not only was I released from the company and its owners, my heart was restored to God's. During the process, a sense of wholeness and completeness was ushered into my life. Quite unexpectedly one day, the impulsive desire to slip a silver chain into my pocket faded away.

That's why the day was so meaningful when Eugene Davidson's name flashed across my computer screen and I felt nothing. I knew I'd been set free.

As followers of Jesus, we're commanded to forgive just as we've been forgiven. Indeed, Jesus says that God's pardon of us is dependent on our forgiving others. God calls us to the life of forgiveness. In forgiving the undeserving, I submit myself to God, and Christ's clemency flows through me.[2]

Such grace emanates through the life of Christ and his death and resurrection. Hanging on the cross, Jesus asks God to forgive those who scorned and abused and robbed him most. The religious leaders. The Roman cohort. The mass of humanity. Even after the resurrection, his first words to the disciples are those of forgiveness. Jesus sends his followers into the world with forgiveness as one of their central missions.[3]

The hard truth I had to face was that unforgiveness ranks

among those things for which I most need God's forgiveness.

Whose name pops up on your computer screen that makes you bristle? Whose picture incites animosity? Who do you sense the Spirit is nudging you to radically forgive?

Thanks to God's work, I don't hold bitterness toward Eugene anymore, but I'm working on forgiving other situations and people now. Eugene was only the beginning of my journey.[4]

Unforgiveness feels like a prison built by the hands of a criminal where we end up incarcerated. Whether robbed, violated, or betrayed, we find ourselves trapped by the bondage of bitterness, the chains of cynicism, and the shackles of sin. With enough time, we can convince ourselves the prisons of our past were built by someone else, but unforgiveness is a cage we construct ourselves. If we choose to stop focusing on our inward pain and instead scan the perimeter, we discover the door to freedom hangs wide open thanks to Christ. The choice is ours.

.009:
MIRACLE ON
THE RUNWAY

The Wonder of Gratitude

A MIDDLE-AGED WOMAN with curly auburn hair limped across the parking lot. I ran to introduce myself. That's when Karen looked up, winced, and offered a modest hello. With unmistakable determination in her eyes, she made her way toward the coffee shop one painstaking step at a time.

Karen's face softened as soon as she sat down. Her countenance transformed, and she budded with vitality. "What do you know about my story?" she asked.

"Only bits and pieces I've heard from your sister," I said. "Though I've been praying since I heard about your family."

Karen flashed through a series of memories. A roommate in college had set her up with David on a blind date. Timid as a big-eyed field mouse, he had only said five sentences the entire night. Karen assumed the evening was a disaster, but David called her the next day. The couple's affections blossomed like a lily. Eighteen months later, they traveled to Florida to scuba dive together. Awed by the colorful corals and the tropical fish, Karen noticed David swimming away from the reef. Puzzled by his interest in what looked like nothing more than rubble and sand, she watched as he picked up a shard of concrete to write the words "Marry Me" on the ocean floor. Three months later they exchanged vows.

David's work as a general contractor building hospitals complemented Karen's work as a nurse. For the next few years, building projects took the young couple around the country before they settled in Colorado to be closer to family.

Karen told me that David was always interested in flying, in part because his brother flew F/A-18 fighter jets. David decided to get his pilot's license. A few years later he began looking into building an aircraft. David asked Karen if he could build the tail of a plane in the garage, assuring her that the whole project would cost less than a thousand dollars. After completing the tail, David wondered if he could build wings for just a few thousand dollars more. The conversation repeated itself over a five-year period until David had built an airplane from the ground up.

Karen acknowledged the way flying had inspired David to become more extroverted. "David was always extremely quiet and reserved," Karen recalled. "But something about flying sparked a wild passion in him. He became more sociable. He joined the flying club. He even became more interactive with coworkers and joined the office fantasy football league."

David took the plane across the country on multiple occasions to visit family and friends. Weekends were spent working on the plane and teaching their son how to fly. "I always gave him a tough time that he never took me!" Karen said. "We always said that when the kids were out of the house, we'd fly together more."

Two weeks shy of their twenty-fifth wedding anniversary, the day finally came when their youngest daughter turned sixteen. The couple decided to leave her with her older brother and fly to Texas to attend their nephew's graduation. The plane took off without incident on a calm blue-sky Colorado morning.

Karen became entranced in her mystery novel until David announced, "Honey! You've got to see this."

The clouds opened as they flew toward them, peeling and splitting to the sides as the aircraft pushed forward. In all their years of flying, neither Karen nor David had ever seen anything like it.

As they neared their destination and the plane approached the runway, Karen sensed David's excitement in seeing his family. Karen glanced at the plane's altimeter. Everything was set for a smooth landing; they were even on time for lunch.

Suddenly, something went terribly wrong. For some unknown reason, the plane dropped. One minute she was looking at the runway, and the next the airplane's wings were brushing the tops of the trees. Karen momentarily lost consciousness.

"No! No! No!" David screamed as the plane banked sharply to the left.

Karen awoke surrounded by wreckage, hanging by the straps of her seat's safety harness. She remembers pushing herself up so she could breathe. She looked over at her husband, his arms extended across her lap possibly in an effort to protect her. He was covered in blood, and she could see a deep gash on his head.

Karen watched as a team of paramedics cut David from the plane first before pulling the engine mount off her leg to remove her. She leaned down and picked up three parts of her foot and ankle held together by connective tissue. She handed them to the paramedic.

Once secured onto the stretcher, they loaded her onto the helicopter. In shock, Karen didn't realize the severity of her injuries.

"Does anyone know about David?" she asked the medics on the helicopter.

No one knew.

Wheeled into the emergency room, Karen felt the chilly metal edge of scissors. A nurse cut off her clothes to assess the injuries. Again she asked, "Does anyone know about David?"

No one knew any details.

In preparation for surgery, Karen was wheeled into X-ray. While the technicians debated the best way to take the images without exacerbating her injuries, Karen learned from an untrained student chaplain that David had passed away. The pain was insufferable—not only from losing her husband but also from the open wound exposing the remaining tendons of her ankle.

Tear-stained, blood-soaked, Karen survived with a pelvis smashed in five places, three cracked ribs, a dislocated clavicle, a severely sprained right ankle, and a shredded and crushed left leg.

After a series of surgeries, the doctors gave Karen an agonizing choice: whether or not to attempt to save her foot. The medical professionals explained that the process of rebuilding the limb would require more than two years without any guarantee of success. The procedure involved multiple surgeries with muscle and skin grafts. The painful recovery meant staying in a rehabilitation center with constant medical supervision.

Or she could have the foot removed.

More than anything, Karen wanted to get home to her children. She elected for the amputation. But the surgery didn't go as well as anticipated. The doctor was unable to close the wound. Karen remained in the hospital three additional weeks before the leg tissue was healthy enough for a skin graft.

After returning home, Karen continued to heal, but when the time came to be fitted with a new leg, the prosthetist noticed the skin graft hadn't healed properly. The graft was painful to touch and folding in on itself, plus bone spurs had resulted from the traumatic nature of the injury. She needed additional surgery before she could walk again.

The surgeon had to remove six more inches of her leg.

Karen eventually received a prosthetic leg, but the issues continued.

She took another sip of her coffee before glancing down at

her foot and announcing, "We're still not done!"

"What do you mean?" I asked.

She pulled up her khaki pant leg to expose the shiny steel metal frame of an artificial limb. "The tissue refuses to heal, so I'm going to have another reconstruction," she told me. "And while I'm in the hospital, I'm going to have my right ankle, which was also damaged in the crash, repaired. I'll come out of this surgery without a leg to stand on."

The joke Karen cracked was meant to be funny, but I was too caught up in the horror to laugh. I inspected the face of someone about to enter another operation that would leave her immobile, a woman whose brow should have been furrowed, her expression marked by anger, her tone rigid and bitter. Instead I observed glitters of levity, gratitude, and joy.

"Considering all you've been through and have yet to go through, you seem in good spirits," I said.

"I'm thankful!" Karen said.

"For what?" I asked.

"For so many things!" she answered, launching into stories of God's presence and provision.

Shortly after David's death, she found herself infused with what she could only describe as "liquid love." She felt the tangible presence of the Holy Spirit supporting and comforting her in the first weeks after the crash. This presence allowed her to have an inner peace that astonished the nurses and helped her to endure the tremendous pain as well as the physical and emotional challenges she faced.

"I found out hundreds of people I did not even know heard about my story and were praying for me," she said. "It's extremely humbling to be the object of so much love and support from fellow Christians."

During this time, Karen sensed God saying, *I had to meet David at the end of a runway. Though you may not understand, that's where it had to be for David and me. Know that I've got him.*

"I am overwhelmed with joy and peace," Karen continued. "Joy because I know David no longer wrestles with the dark struggles of this world; peace because I know whose hands hold him."

Karen explained that she prayed for her husband's salvation since they first met. "I know David is with God," she said, beaming with gratitude, "even if it had to come at the end of a runway."

Despite the medical complications, the innumerable bills, the deep grieving, Karen said the penetrating shroud of peace has not left her. The Holy Spirit continues to affirm, *I've got you. I'm carrying you.*

She said that when the pressure of medical bills became more than she could bear, an unmarked envelope with money arrived in the mail. Several coworkers raised a thousand dollars by selling cookbooks. A person at church felt compelled to give Karen a check—unknowingly for the exact amount of an unexpected medical bill.

Miracles weren't solely found in provision but also in the transformation in other people's lives. One friend felt so compelled to support Karen, she organized her own fundraiser and partnered with a local church. In the process, the friend's faith grew to the point where she became a follower of Jesus.

Yet Karen seemed most grateful for her ability to return to work. A licensed lactation consultant, she teaches newborns with eating problems to attach to their mothers. A woman who experienced loss in her life spends her days helping others lay hold of life.

"I see my job as a gift," Karen said. "I want to make a difference. Having a job where I witness the miracle of life each day is one of the things that keeps me going."

"After all you've been through, you're *still* thankful?" I asked.

"I know I've lost a leg," Karen answered. "But even in this I'm grateful. I've gained a freedom I've never had before. I was a fearful child, and now the fear is gone. I see my fearlessness rubbing off on people."

"How do you do it?"

"People say I'm a strong woman, but I'm not. Stubborn maybe, but not strong. When you have nothing, you finally have both hands free to hold on to God."

Karen's story left me speechless, taken aback by her composure and rootedness. Her sense of thankfulness in the midst of so much loss left me wonderstruck. She displayed the wonder of gratitude in regal form.

Her words reminded me of the apostle Paul's. Writing to the church in Thessalonica, he instructs them to express gratitude at all times. Paul writes, "Rejoice always; pray without ceasing; *in everything give thanks;* for this is God's will for you in Christ Jesus."[1]

The mark of a Christian who strives for a vibrant relationship with God is joy, prayer, and gratitude. These are not one-time offerings but perpetual and ongoing expressions—for every situation, in all circumstances—rooted in the will of God and given as gifts by God.

Paul never suggests that believers deny the grief or pain that adversity brings but rather that they recognize, even in the midst of hardship, God's spirit infusing them with joy. Such mirth can't be self-produced; it is a gift of God and evidence of the Spirit.[2] This unexplainable joy is one of the hallmarks of those who follow Christ, setting them apart from many religions, both ancient and modern.

Paul's second instruction is to pray continually. Prayer isn't limited to a particular time of day or formality but is designed to be accessible and constant. Calling on God is designed for both grave and grandiose occasions—an expression meant to become as natural as breathing. Paul prayed for those in Thessalonica regularly and asked them to keep him in their prayers, confident that such a life of prayer shifts perspective from inward to outward, from our own concerns to the needs of others. Constant prayer also expresses our ongoing dependence on God. When woven with happy wonderment, prayer becomes an opportunity to rejoice through adoration and worship.

His final exhortation is to give thanks in all circumstances. Scripture doesn't explicitly say who is to be given thanks, but it's understood as being given to God. Unlike the previous exhortations to practice "always" and "without ceasing," Paul assigns gratitude in "every circumstance," even those that seem undeserving of thanks. In other words, the focus isn't on expressing gratitude every moment but in the midst of every situation—despite the ease or difficulty of the circumstances.[3]

Gratitude doesn't curry favor with God as it does in other pagan religions. Rather than try to gain status through verbal offerings, gratitude invites us to trust God in all things. Thankfulness is the acknowledgment that God can redeem every situation and make us more than triumphant in any circumstance.[4] Whether we're facing a season of absence or abundance, barrenness or bounty, turmoil or tranquility, the command to give thanks remains. To the outsider, such an act is undeserved; but for those who place their faith in God, thankfulness is a powerful confession that God's purpose is being worked out in all things.

The history of the region around Thessalonica reveals even more of the potency of Paul's exhortation. One night while staying in the port city of Troas, Paul receives a vision in which a man from Macedonia summons him, saying, "Come . . . and help us."[5] In response, Paul joins a group to cross the Aegean Sea and share the gospel throughout the region. The team makes their way through Amphipolis and Apollonia to the coastal city of Thessalonica, known for its strategic location and natural resources. The surrounding mountains offered timber for development, a nearby plain provided fertile soil for agriculture; the land proffered wealth through precious metals—the gold, the silver, the iron, the lead. When the Roman soldiers overtook the region, including Thessalonica, they stripped the people and the territory of everything valuable. The booty was so great the Thessalonians were excused from direct taxation for the next hundred years.[6]

After pillaging resources, Rome established a series of economic measures—including prohibiting trade between districts in the region—that impoverished the people. When these laws eventually relaxed, the economic situation in Thessalonica improved. Jobs were created; the majority of the population found work. But some never recovered. One anthology recounts the story of Aristides, a poor man who tallied his great wealth. He called his single sheep a flock, his only cow a herd. Then a wolf killed the sheep and the cow died giving birth. Soon after, he took his life.[7]

The story illustrates the dire financial situation some were facing when Paul penned his letter to the church at Thessalonica—a situation not too different from today. Many found work and financial stability; others struggled to survive. Paul encourages the people in the church to look beyond socioeconomic differences and display love to one another.

When Paul commands the Thessalonians to give thanks in all circumstances, he knows the historical baggage they carry. During his previous visit, he undoubtedly saw the disparity of wealth, the injustices of the authorities, the pangs of poverty, yet he still instructs them to express gratitude.

Maybe because he, too, learned the importance of giving thanks in all circumstances.

The book of Acts unveils some details of Paul's journeys. Shortly after receiving the vision that Paul should come to Macedonia, Paul and Silas are stalked by a slave girl who has a spirit of divination. Annoyed by the girl's proclamations, Paul commands the spirit to leave her. The girl's owners discover she can no longer practice fortune-telling. They falsely accuse Paul and Silas of civil disturbance then beat them bloody.

Paul and his companion are thrown into prison. An earthquake opens the doors of the prison. Soon after, the prison guard becomes a follower of Jesus. Paul and Silas are then freed to continue their journey. When they arrive in Thessalonica, Paul finds a synagogue where he explains the death and resurrection of Jesus Christ to the locals. While some believe—including God-fearing Greeks and women—the Jews form a mob, setting the city into an uproar. Paul and his fellow travelers are forced to leave the city, but adversity continues to follow wherever he goes.

Over the course of his life, Paul is tossed into prison and brutally beaten on multiple occasions, shipwrecked, and nearly drowned. Falsely accused, surrounded by thieves, his life is marked by affliction and controversy, his body shaped by exhaustion, thirst, and hunger. Yet even in the midst of life's heaviest blows, he still says give thanks. If Paul lived a safe, comfortable life, his words could easily be dismissed. But Paul embodied his message.

Paul doesn't just say give thanks, but give thanks *in all circumstances*, in everything. The wonder arises when we express gratitude in situations that appear to deserve none. When Paul and Silas find themselves in prison, instead of sighing, they sing.[8] This is where the message is difficult to swallow. Paul doesn't say give thanks in some things or good things but in everything— even when it seems impossible.

I'm often grateful for the good, but the wonder comes when we thank God in the midst of the bad. Paul doesn't say give thanks *for* everything but *in* everything. That's what Karen learned to do. She didn't thank God *for* the plane crash but *in* the midst of the aftermath. The wonder of gratitude isn't found in saying thanks for *good* things but in *all* things—including the bad.

Leaving the coffee shop that day, I marveled at Karen's story. In the past, I'd met people who masquerade as sanguine, but just below the surface, they lived in unspeakable pain. Karen was the opposite. Though the chronic pain was palpable, just below the surface, she radiated joy.

"Though giving thanks in everything seems like an insurmountable task, God equips us if we allow him," she told me, her words echoing in my mind. "It's a gift we receive through his grace and supernatural power."

Something about Karen's story haunted me—in a good way. Like the enjoyment that comes from sitting under a tree on a sunny day, Karen's abounding gratitude shaded my perspective in the most unexpected way. That evening I could still see the glimmer in Karen's eyes whenever I closed mine for a moment. Sitting on the couch in the silence, I flipped open my Bible to Psalm 13, which begins with an unflinching address of God: "How long, O LORD? Will You forget me forever? How long will You hide Your face from me? How long shall I take counsel in my soul, having sorrow in my heart all the day? How long will my enemy be exalted over me?"[9]

The psalmist uses the timeless cry of humanity, *How long?* to summon God. After rousing God through complaint, the indictment shifts to a petition: "Consider and answer me, O LORD my God; enlighten my eyes, or I will sleep the sleep of death, and my enemy will say, 'I have overcome him.' And my adversaries will rejoice when I am shaken."[10]

A confession of pain is followed by a request for God to act. Listen. Speak. Vindicate. Rescue. Sustain. Protect. All these are hinted at in the psalmist's petition for God's intervention, namely, that the Lord will bring deliverance. Without God, all hope is lost.

Then, with the ever-powerful word *but,* the psalmist makes a startling sharp turn toward praise and thanksgiving. "But I have trusted in Your lovingkindness; my heart shall rejoice in Your salvation. I will sing to the LORD, because He has dealt bountifully with me."[11]

Confidence in God replaces complaint, which leads to rejoicing. The cornerstone of the psalmist's refrain is found in the loving-kindness of God. Fresh gratitude is found in God's goodness and never-ending love. Six short verses are all that's needed to transport the psalmist from the bowels of despair to the peaks of praise. That's the beauty of gratitude: it invites us to a shift in our relationship with God and others. We're invited to journey from loss to trust, from pain to praise.

That thankful disposition plays an essential role because it invites us to reorient our lives toward God. Through praise and thanksgiving, we reflect on the transcendent nature of God— the reality that he is above all. As we look up toward God, we also can't help but be reminded of our smallness. This shift in perspective softens our hearts, inviting us once again to lean into God's goodness, to look up for his salvation.

How do your circumstances affect your attitude of thanksgiving toward your life and God? In what areas of your life do you tend to hold back expressions of thanks? Will you answer the call to give thanks no matter what situation you're facing?

Karen embodied the wonder of gratitude like no one I'd ever met before. She found joy in great pain, hope in despair, peace in uncertainty. Still weeks away from another surgery, she radiated thankfulness in the wreckage of life. That kind of gratitude makes me curious to know God more. Karen's thankfulness was not for the circumstances but in the God who refused to leave her side. Such gratefulness is pure madness. Nothing in the realm of logic makes it possible. Only God. Karen's gratitude wasn't natural but supernatural. And her appreciativeness left me undone.

Karen taught me that when we live life awake to the wonder of God around us, we find reason to give thanks even in the wake of wreckage and discover God at the end of the runway.

.010:
THE LEGEND OF
CACTUS JACK

The Wonder of Abundant Life

THEY CALLED HIM CACTUS JACK. Sky-blue eyes and a silver goatee reminiscent of the spiny desert plant sat atop his tall frame accentuated by leathery skin that spoke of a lifetime spent in outdoor adventure. Like most people, Cactus Jack clocked a forty-hour workweek, but unlike most people, he logged his hours as a professional poker player.

Well into his eighties, Cactus Jack discovered cards as an effective means of supplementing Social Security. Five days a week, he drove from his home in Saint George, Utah, across the border into Nevada, where legalized gambling formed the backbone of the state's economy. He preferred the rugged gambling town of Mesquite to the glitter of Las Vegas.

Poker wasn't a financial risk for Cactus Jack as much as a complex mathematical calculation. He kept his advice to young players simple: pay attention to the cards, keep track of your odds, never let your emotions get involved. Over the years, Cactus Jack won far more than he lost and stored his winnings in a black sock beside his bed. His stash of cash paid for prescriptions, groceries, and gas for his daily commute.

Jack was a regular fixture at the card table for more than two decades. His unique fashion choices certified him as a bona fide character. He loved to wear a white cowboy hat with light-colored three-piece suits and crocodile boots. A well-chewed, unlit cigar hung from the right side of his mouth. Every few weeks, he strutted into the casino with a woman on his arm. His wife of sixty-plus years, Martha, wore long flowery muumuus and carried a sixty-four-ounce trucker's cup jingling with silver coins. When Cactus Jack disappeared into the poker room, Martha paused to pray in front of a row of slot machines before taking a seat on one of the faux-leather stools.

His presence at the casino was as steady as the desert heat during the summer. Whenever he didn't appear, friends at the casino knew something was wrong. On such occasions, dealers and fellow players phoned Jack's house. Sometimes Cactus Jack took a substantive loss in the poker room and needed time to recalibrate his emotions before returning. Other times he or Martha nursed an illness. Upon hearing the news, someone from the casino would drop off chicken soup or a homemade pie.

Eventually, Martha couldn't make the trek anymore because her health deteriorated as she progressed through her seventies. Cactus Jack stayed home for months to care for her until she died.

When he returned to the casino, everyone—from the poker dealers to the players—noticed the sparkle in his eye had vanished with Martha.

Cactus Jack continued his commute to Mesquite until, without warning, he disappeared from the casino for more than a week. Phone calls from concerned friends poured in. People soon learned that Cactus Jack had died from heart trauma.

My mother struggled to deliver the news.

After all, Cactus Jack was my grandfather.

Leif and I, along with my mother and aunt, traveled to Saint George once we learned my grandfather was in the hospital. He died before any of us arrived. In the wake of his death, we began the long process of sorting through his possessions, which felt like following a creaky staircase into a bottomless vault of memories.

Each of us tackled different rooms throughout the house. Dusty shelves, jammed drawers, eclectic artwork, and odd thingamabobs met us everywhere we turned. My favorite discovery was a collection of plaques and trophies from the 1950s celebrating Grandpa's world records in speedboat racing. Because several of the competition classes were eliminated, he still holds a few records today.

Underneath Cactus Jack's bed, I unearthed a dusty stack of

photos in an empty cigar box. Sorting through the old images, I recognized a sandy-blonde girl with sun-kissed cheeks as my mom. She had grown up on the shores of Englewood Beach, Florida, where my grandparents managed a resort and sold real estate. The photos showed my mom and her three siblings holding up an enormous snook. One photo captured Mom pinching with pride a black shark's tooth she had found on the beach; another presented my aunts and uncle as kids gathered around the table for a Thanksgiving feast.

In the overflow of the garage, a set of golf clubs reminded me what had brought my grandparents to southern Utah years before. My grandparents owned a cabin on the shore of Henry's Lake near Yellowstone National Park, but the frigid temperatures made the winters unbearable. They longed for a place where they could still play eighteen holes during the coldest months of the year. Their solution was to divide their time between Utah and Idaho.

Many of the junky items alluded to my grandparents' final years when they watched too many hours of the Home Shopping Network and ordered unneeded treasures off infomercials. Though their grandchildren had long since entered adulthood, I found handfuls of plastic toys, stuffed animals, and wacky gizmos. Somehow aging awoke my grandparents' childlike passion for play.

As we sorted through trash and treasure, my mom retold classic Cactus Jack stories. One year, when business was slow, she said, he built a palm-frond beach shack near Englewood Beach. The novelty real estate office caught the attention of tourists and provided an upsurge in home buying.

Mom reminded me of a pivotal moment in my grandfather's life: When a friend asked my great-grandfather for a loan to start a small grocery store, my great-grandfather gave his friend the money. The store took off. The friend told my great-grandfather that he could have his money back or gamble on the investment in exchange for a percentage of the business. My great-grandfather took back his money.

That grocery store became a large grocery-store chain known today as Publix.[1]

Such were the real-life lessons Grandpa watched unfold during his adolescence that undoubtedly shaped his outlook toward taking risks.

One of my fondest memories was fishing with Grandpa as a child. We'd wake up early in the morning, bathe in bug spray, and then sit together in the early morning silence waiting for the slightest tug on our lines. My grandfather knew live worms gave me the willies so he baited my hook every time. Whenever we brought home trout, grandma smoked and canned the fish. All these years later, I still can't eat smoked fish without thinking about my grandfather.

I also remembered the assignment I received early in my career to interview the televangelist John Hagee. Grandpa acted as if I'd laid down a royal flush for all the chips. This was a brush with fame from his perspective; he asked me to share details of the interview at least seventeen times. I never understood my grandfather's enthusiasm for the televangelist, but his passion revealed his own desire to know God.

Even Leif chimed in with a few Grandpa stories. The first time Leif visited my grandparents, Cactus Jack pulled out a deck of cards and began dealing. Grandpa tapped the top of the deck and asked, "What are the odds of the next card being a face card or higher?"

Leif stared at him blankly. Cactus Jack explained the cumbersome math equations needed to calculate the probabilities of the top card. Not bad for an eighty-four-year-old.

Emptying dozens of bottles of prescription medication from my grandfather's bathroom revealed how much his health had deteriorated over the last three years before his death. During a previous visit, I had noted how his athletic stroll had been reduced into an old-man shuffle. Cactus Jack found comfort from the aches and pains and indignities of aging through a self-prescribed blend of cigars, sugar, and cable news—all of which are manageable on their own, but when combined, produce a potentially explosive situation room.

As consistent as the sunrise, Grandpa's day always began with Fox News. As daily headlines broke, Grandpa self-medicated with donuts and a bowl of jelly beans he kept nearby—both of which welcomed him closer to the no man's land of diabetic coma. To help him stay awake, he slipped on his oxygen mask, lit his stogie, and crowed muffled obscenities at the news anchors whenever a debate riled him.

Watching the disturbing scene unfold, we hung our heads, knowing that no amount of cajoling was going to pry the bear claw pastry, remote control, or lighter from Grandpa's grasp. Instead, we decided to take bets on what would kill Grandpa first.

Dusting, scrubbing, cleaning, and sorting filled our days. Sometimes a sound would emerge from someone in another room. A drawer stuffed with knickknacks usually brought a groan; a wacky toy brought laughter. The white cowboy hat brought everyone together as we paused to admire my grandfather's signature accessory. But the work also stirred up deep emotions. Watching tears run down my mom's and aunt's faces made me want to be a source of strength and stability. Every time I felt a rush of emotion, I widened my eyes, increasing the surface tension so I didn't have to feel soggy. Then I slipped into a nearby room and wiped away any escapees.

Sometime during the afternoon of the third day, I couldn't contain my grief any longer. I disappeared into the guest bedroom and wept. The tears flowed freely, leaving my eyes bloodshot, my face swollen. When I reemerged, I returned to sorting through bookshelves, but my mother caught a glimpse of my face. I acknowledged the process felt overwhelming but assured her I was fine—even if I wasn't 100 percent honest.

My aunt returned one day carrying a black plastic canister the size of a coffee can. "Here's Grandpa!" she said.

Taken aback by the announcement, I realized I'd never seen someone's remains after they returned from the crematorium. I held out my hands as if I were reaching for a newborn. Clutching the box, I was surprised by its weight. A gentle shake of the container reminded me of the finality of life.

Grandpa had come home. Now we deliberated over what to do with him. My aunt suggested we place him on top of the piano, where we could imagine him watching us as we cleaned. In some families, this might seem ridiculous, but in my family, it was perfectly in line with how we handle our grief. Still, even for me—fully initiated into our unique familial dynamics—the whole experience felt surreal and strange, and I disappeared into a back bedroom to weep for a second time.

Though I kept my mourning to myself, my mom and aunt felt freer to well up with emotion. After much discussion, they decided that one of them would spread Grandpa's ashes near Grandma's remains at their home in Idaho the following summer. Instead of a formal funeral, we'd celebrate Grandpa's life by inviting a few of his friends to attend church together. The idea struck me as unusual, but it couldn't be stranger than having a professional-poker-playing, speedboat-world-record-setting grandfather.

On Sunday morning, I buckled in for the drive to church then unclicked the seatbelt and bounded out of the car. "What are you doing?" my mother asked.

"If this is the closest thing I'm going to get to attending a funeral for my grandfather, then I think he should be there!" I said. I ran back inside the house and grabbed Grandpa's black plastic canister.

My mother and aunt glanced at each other as we backed down the driveway. Sitting in the backseat with Grandpa on my lap, my mind replayed scenes from *Weekend at Bernie's*, the 1980s dark comedy about two employees who try to convince everyone their boss is still alive by carrying his corpse around with them.

When we arrived at church, I realized I didn't have an appropriate carrier for Grandpa. I managed to slide him into my aunt's purse before Grandpa's friends surrounded us. Betty, an eighty-something pal, boasted curlicue white hair and a sugary-sweet disposition. Irene, a weathered seventy-something poker player from the casino, explained that she had played countless hands of poker with Grandpa over the years. Her eyes welled up every time Cactus Jack's name was mentioned. Dorothy, a sixty-something blackjack dealer, sported a form-fitting, black nylon dress. Each one of these women greeted me with a hug and spoke of the kindnesses my grandfather had showed them.

The service opened with a hymn then paused to welcome new visitors. We introduced ourselves. The pastor acknowledged my grandfather's support of the church and offered his condolences. Then he invited the congregation to join in singing another hymn. During the Scripture reading, I pulled Grandpa out of my aunt's satchel and sat him next to me on the pew. I figured Grandpa should sit in his favorite pew in the back one last time. Knowing his colorful, nontraditional character, I have a hunch he would have smiled at the scene.

The pastor delivered a short sermon on the resurrected Christ. As he spoke, I found comfort in knowing Grandpa was in the presence of Jesus. I imagined Jesus open-armed, my grandfather wide-eyed at his first face-to-face encounter. Glancing down the pew at the motley crew of gamblers, casino employees, and one woman easily mistaken for a hussy, I was bashed broadside: these were the exact people Jesus embraced. The love and grace of God didn't discriminate. Considering those who played blackjack with Cactus Jack, it's easy to understand how the invitation to experience the abundant life of Christ extends to all.

We returned home the next day. Over the next few weeks, my mind drifted back to my grandfather. Even with his flaws and unconventional life, Cactus Jack had passionately answered the call to become a follower of Christ. Scenes of my grandfather duck hunting and smoking trout flashed through my mind. I breathed in the memory of the stale cigar smell of my grandparents' motor home that was always parked in their driveway. Slathered in Jesus-festival bumper stickers, the rusty beast had traveled nearly two hundred thousand miles traversing the country before finally being sold for scrap metal.

I cherish the memory of my grandparents' large-print Bible, which always sat beside their bed. Nearly every page was marked up with illegible comments and underlined phrases. Once I opened the Bible upright, and a cascade of photos, letters, and notes from family members fluttered to the floor like confetti. Each note and image reminded my grandparents to pray for us as they read and studied the Bible. I could almost hear my grandfather walking around the house humming hymns blaring from their eight-track-tape player.

Etched into my mind is also my grandparents' generosity. Every day their mailbox overflowed with solicitations for donations from orphanages, overseas outreaches, nonprofits serving the poor. They received more free address labels from ministries than anyone I've ever known. I once asked my grandmother why they seemed to be on every ministry's mailing list.

"Because we support them all," my grandmother told me.

"Why do you do that?" I asked, shocked by their readiness to give despite their limited income.

"Sometimes we can only send them five or ten dollars, but we always manage to send something," she said matter-of-factly. "God's always provided for us, so we need to help provide for others."

After the church service, one of Grandpa's friends leaned over and said, "Your grandmother led more people to Christ at the slot machines than any woman I've ever known."

Her comment made me realize that both my grandparents had left a legacy of love in what some would consider low places.

My grandfather didn't just color outside the lines of life, he scribbled outside them, too, but in the process he laid hold of God and helped others do the same. Growing up, I often heard stories about my grandfather's behavior at the poker table. While other players were foul-mouthed and demeaning of the casino staff, my grandfather was a gentleman—courteous and considerate of everyone. His kind behavior earned him the opportunity to share his faith with others. On multiple occasions, he ended a poker match with a fellow player accepting Christ. My grandmother managed to transform a slot machine into a pulpit of sorts, inviting strangers to entrust their lives to someone greater than Lady Luck.

As I thought about my grandfather, I realized he didn't *just* live, he *truly* lived.

In the Gospel of John, Jesus said, "The thief comes only to steal and kill and destroy; I came that they may have life, and have it abundantly."[2] The abundant life begins when we choose to live our lives for God. We experience this fullness as we discover facets of God's character through Scripture, encounter his faithful presence in our daily lives, and respond to God's voice as he leads and directs us. The abundant life begins here on earth as we choose to align our whole selves with God and continues as we abide with God forever. The eternal abundant life we're called to starts now and never ends.

Though I had studied the theological and heady meaning behind Christ's promise of full life, in my imperfect grandfather, I saw the abundance lived out. Rather than become distracted by the fear of that which steals, kills, and destroys, my grandfather focused his attention on the One who came to bring life. He tackled each day with the hopeful anticipation that God would bring good things, and even if he didn't, God remained good.

Reflecting on my grandfather's life, I can't help but think of how many of us fail to embrace the abundant life Christ promises. Focusing on our areas of weakness or imperfection, we convince ourselves that we're outside the realm of being used by God.

We lose sight of the long line of biblical men and women who followed God, even changing history, despite blemishes on their records, flaws in their character. We gloss over the details: Rahab lived sultry and David committed adultery; Abraham lied, Peter denied, Jacob vied; once the weather turned fine, Noah turned to wine; Thomas doubted, Martha pouted, Elijah spouted. Somewhere along the way, the rhyme overtakes our reason: we forget that history is filled with God using imperfect, broken people to accomplish his will and bring glory to his name.

And that gives me great hope.

Such a legacy isn't a hall pass to live a defective life but a wild invitation to embrace the abundant life—seeking God in every situation, sharing the good news wherever we find ourselves, and never sitting on the sidelines of the grand experience of living.

Instead of cruising through life, my grandfather left this world wholly spent, coasting on fumes from a life fully lived. Grandpa made many mistakes, but he never failed to celebrate the grandeur of life and the earnestness of living. Cactus Jack refused to live sleepy. Instead, he embarked each day wide-eyed to the possibilities. He discovered the wonder of the abundant life, and the legacy he gave me is one I want to lay hold of—loving God and others, taking risks, trying new things, learning to find joy in each day as a gift.

Cactus Jack embraced the life many are afraid to live. Too many of us play and pray it safe. We allow our aspirations to stay in our heads, our goals to remain barely outside our grasp. Life becomes a series of unrealized hopes and dreams. Rather than engage in the fullness of life, we remain on the sidelines and pass up uncounted opportunities. Our fears become greater than the hope of the One who came to bring us abundant life.

What is keeping you on the sidelines of life? What have you

convinced yourself is impossible with God? Where have you allowed fear to replace faith? What's stopping you from moving forward? Or taking your first step toward change? Even if you stumble, you may find your dream expanding into something even more enchanting than you ever imagined.

I needed to stop mourning the loss of my grandfather's life and start celebrating the life my grandfather lived. Cactus Jack laid hold of his dreams and left this world having given everything. And that kind of life, the abundant kind, was worth celebrating. I knew I needed to throw a party.

More than a year later, I drove down to the local bakery to pick up a birthday cake I had special ordered. I noticed the baker's befuddled expression as he brought a large box to the counter. He took a second look at me before opening the lid.

"This what you wanted?" he asked.

I nodded. Next to a silver slot machine sat five cards revealing a royal flush—each heart reflective of my love for my grandfather. Below the unbeatable poker hand were the words "Happy Birthday, Cactus Jack" in lime-green icing.

Returning home, I worked alongside Leif to prepare the last few appetizers. Soon my friends arrived for the untraditional celebration. Halfway through the party, I paused to make a toast to my grandfather.

Then I grabbed a handful of tortilla chips from the bowl on our living room table, looked across the crowded room of friends, and thought, *This is the way he would have wanted it.*

BONUS TRACKS

THIRTY DAYS
OF WONDER

A Challenge to Experience God More

I'VE SHARED MY JOURNEYS WITH YOU hoping to inspire you to experience God more for yourself. As followers of Jesus, we have the opportunity to live each day in wild amazement of God. If we pay attention, we can begin discovering the wonders all around us—those moments of spiritual awakening that spark our curiosity to know God more.

If the desire to encounter God's wonder has been stirred inside of you, consider picking up a copy of the *Wonderstruck Bible Study* (Lifeway) as a companion to this challenge so you can more fully experience the wonder alongside others.

Here's your challenge: Over the next month, find a friend who will commit to praying for wonder each day and then together live alert to the ways God answers. That means that over the next thirty days, you may sense the Holy Spirit leading you to do and say things you may have passed by before. You may find God nudging you to reach out to someone you've never noticed. You may feel an urge that the person who is supposed to volunteer or get involved is *you*. Or you may sense the tug of the Holy Spirit to take more time diving into the Scriptures or taking time to pray. You may begin sensing God's presence in places and experiences that you never expected.

The great news is that you can share what you're discovering online. Beginning on the first day of each month, a new group of men and women from around the world are going to be praying for wonder. They're going to ask God to open their spiritual eyes to his goodness and presence in fresh ways, and you can join them! The conversation will take place on my Facebook page (facebook.com/margaretfeinberg) as well as on Twitter (@mafeinberg) and Pinterest (pinterest.com/mafeinberg). We're inviting you to post your experiences, your aha moments, and your photos that display what you're discovering along the way. With each post, simply use hashtag #livewonderstruck and look for others who are on the same journey with you.

To help guide you through this month, a different activity is provided for each day. Be sensitive to the Holy Spirit with each activity—you may find a few that you sense God nudging you to spend several days practicing and experiencing. Each night, you may find it helpful to preview the next day's activity so you wake up ready and expectant to discover the wonder.

Day 1: Reflection

The wonders of God surround you. Prayerfully spend some time reflecting on those things that prevent you from awakening to the wonder of God. Write them down, and then ask God to remove those obstacles that prevent you from experiencing him more. Ask God to make you supernaturally aware of the Spirit's presence and leading over the next thirty days. Consider sharing online some of the obstacles you wrestle with. (#livewonderstruck)

Day 2: Time

Reflect on the wondrous gift of time. Pull out a calendar or day planner and spend fifteen minutes considering all that's on your schedule for the upcoming two weeks. Consider marking which activities fill up your time versus those that fill you with life and provide opportunities to awaken to the wonder of God all around. Prayerfully consider what changes—including cuts and additions you need to make to your schedule—to awaken yourself to the wonder of rest and a healthy rhythm in your daily life. Make sure you have time built into each day for the remaining days of the challenge.

Day 3: Beauty

Look for wonder through a camera lens throughout the day. Carry a camera or your camera-equipped cell phone to snap photos of God's beauty, grace, love, peace, and joy all around you. Share these beautiful moments of wonder with others—online or in person. Upload and use the hashtag #livewonderstruck.

Day 4: *Hope*

Nothing awakens wonder inside us like breathing hope into the hopeless. This morning ask God to awaken you to someone who others have given up on. Prayerfully consider how God may want to use you to impart hope and encouragement in this person's life. As you drive down the block, consider each neighbor. As you pass through a downtown area, consider every person hustling to and from work. As you walk through a park, consider the single parents playing with their children. Ask God to rouse you to the needs of those around you and use you to bring the wonder of restoration to others.

Day 5: Creation

Creation beckons us to open our eyes to the wonders of God. Look for a place outside where all you can see is God's creation. If you're in an urban area, consider visiting a park and lying down under a tree where all you can see is its branches and slivers of sky above. Spend fifteen minutes simply sitting or resting in that place. Pay attention to the details—the textures, the colors, the intricate care with which God formed creation. Allow yourself to spontaneously respond to God in thanks and worship, celebrating the wonders of creation all around.

Day 6: Forgiveness

Unforgiveness holds us back from fully experiencing God's wonder. Sometimes the hardest person to forgive is yourself. Take fifteen minutes to prayerfully consider any things for which you've had a hard time forgiving yourself. Record them on a blank sheet of paper. Then take a few moments to forgive yourself for each one. After you forgive yourself, rip up the sheet of paper as a sign of keeping no record of wrongs. Allow yourself to celebrate the forgiveness God offers you through Jesus. You are a wondrous child of God! Spend some time thanking God for the way he created you and the redemptive work he's doing in your life, and walk in the wonder of forgiveness.

Day 7: Silence

God often chooses to reveal the wonder of himself in quiet moments. Sit in silence for twenty unbroken minutes. Set an alarm, if need be, so you know how much time has passed. Keep paper and pen nearby to write down any fluttering thoughts. Embrace the silence then invite God to speak. Reflect on what you hear in this posture of listening. Pray that God reminds you of people for whom you can pray. Ask God to bring scriptures to mind that he wants you to consider. Enjoy the wondrous silence of just being in God's presence.

Day 8: Relationship

In choosing to be fully present with someone, we can experience many wonders. Spend a few moments reflecting on your schedule for the day. Who could you spend a half-hour or hour with and be fully present, fully yourself? Maybe you have a coworker you could invite to lunch. Or one of your children whom you haven't been able to give full attention to lately. Find a place and a time—whether it's in your dining room or living room or a park or coffee shop—where you can be fully yourself and warm your soul in the glow of both knowing and being known.

Day 9: Sky

God's sanctuary in the sky awaits us all. Take fifteen minutes to look, *really look,* at all the lights in the sky—the disc that is the moon, the Milky Way, the stars, even the planes that shoot across night's canopy. Even if there's light pollution, take note of the shadows and the textures above. As you observe the lights—

those created by God and others crafted by humankind—reflect on the promise God made to Abraham thousands of years ago that his descendants would be more numerous than all the stars in the sky (Genesis 15:5). Consider God's faithfulness in your own life and journey.

Day 10: Stillness

Wonders await in the stillness. Depending on the time of year, prepare a cup of hot peppermint tea or pour a glass of sweet tea. Fill a mug with dark hot chocolate and marshmallows or open a can of Cheerwine—whatever your favorite beverage may be. Then find a quiet room, a comfortable chair, and sit still for twenty minutes. Your only movement should be nestling into the chair and occasionally sipping your beverage. Allow yourself to be fully present in the moment—aware of your hands, your feet, your spine, every aspect of your body's position. In this place of pausing, talk to God. Tell him what's really on your heart and mind. Share with him things you've been afraid to say aloud. Give yourself wholly and fully to God in prayer and experience the wonder.

Day 11: Dream

Some of God's greatest wonders await us when we allow ourselves to dream. Spend twenty minutes today creating a list of things you'd like to see God do in your life and the lives of those around you. Write down things you'd do, places you'd visit, and situations you'd encounter if anything were possible. Ask God to lift the lid off your prayer life and begin believing him for things you previously thought impossible. Walk boldly in the wonder of divine expectation.

Day 12: Prayer

Wonder awaits us in our prayer lives. Set aside twenty minutes today to talk to God, but instead of conversing with God as you normally do, consider limiting prayers to three words each. Take note of the challenges and joys you experience. Reflect on what it means to be intentional with each word as you lift your praises and petitions to God and rediscover the wonder of prayer.

Day 13: Letter

Gratitude provides the opportunity to celebrate the breadth and depth of God's wonder. Take twenty minutes today to write a letter to God—maybe even a love letter. Express your affections to God. Thank him for all that he's done for you and all that he has yet to do. Thank him for those big and little and long forgotten things and allow your soul to dance in the wonders of gratitude.

Day 14: You

Life is one of God's greatest wonders. Much of your life is spent giving, serving, and working. But today the challenge is to do something that makes you—just you—feel rejuvenated, refreshed, and brings you joy. A high-energy sports activity. A meal at your favorite bistro. An hour of knitting or enjoying your favorite craft. A coffee date with a friend. A great novel. Spend at least thirty minutes—but preferably one hour—doing something today that makes you grateful to be alive and rediscover the abundant life that awaits you each and every day.

Day 15: Sunrise

God's wonder meets all of humanity at dawn, but we often sleep through it unaware. This morning set your alarm to awake before sunrise. You can check online to find out what time the sun will poke its head above the horizon where you live. Before you nod off to sleep, ask God to reveal himself to you in a meaningful way in the morning. As you awake and watch, pay attention to the first shafts of light. Observe the softness of dawn, the hues of the sun's first rays, the illumination and beauty all around you. Lamentations 3:22–23 says the Sunrise Maker's loving-kindness "is new every morning." Spend some time reflecting on how God has displayed this truth not just in the sunrise but throughout your life. Let the wonder of God's creation break through your soul like the morning's first rays. And don't forget to thank God for meeting you this morning.

Day 16: Rest

Apart from rest, we can sleep through the wonders of God. Though your schedule may be full, consider what you can do today to imbibe rest as one of God's greatest gifts. Perhaps you can sneak in a catnap. Or allow your eyes to rest midafternoon. Or climb into bed an hour early. Look for twenty minutes or more when you can just rest—allowing your mind and body and emotions to recalibrate. Drink in rest to awaken more fully to the wonders of God all around.

Day 17: God

Wondrous delight is found in the presence of God. With a blank sheet of paper and pen in hand, along with a Bible nearby, begin making a list of the characteristics of God. Write down various names for God. Record attributes of God. List promises of God. Then spend some time thanking God simply for who he is and offering words of adoration to him. The wonder of God's presence awaits you.

Day 18: Restore

Portraits of restoration surround us, but sometimes we walk by such beautiful work unaware. Look around your home for something that needs restoring. A wall that needs touch-up paint. A piece of jewelry that's lost its shine. An appliance that needs to be fixed. A piece of furniture that needs to be refinished. Instead of waiting another day, begin the process of repair today. As you work, consider the wondrous work of restoration that God has done and is doing in your life.

Day 19: Appreciation

People are often the couriers of God's wonder in our lives. Take some time to look around. Make a list of the people who have made a difference in your life. Express your gratitude to three of them. Pick up the phone. Send an email. Write a handwritten note. Whatever form of expression you choose, know that as you express your appreciation, you'll be encouraging them to continue serving and helping others. Sit back and watch the wonder of gratitude unfold as you love those who mean the most to you.

Day 20: Vacation

When we choose to get away by ourselves or with others—even for a half-day or overnight stay—we rediscover God's wonders as we recalibrate our lives through a shift in perspective. Today is the day to plan that getaway you've really been meaning to take. Talk to your roommate or spouse. Find a babysitter or pet sitter. Call your family. Text your friends. And set the date for a mini-vacation. You don't have to spend much money. You don't have to go far. You can enjoy a "staycation" by reserving a night at a local hotel or even pitching a tent in your own back yard. Don't wait another day to schedule a break and enjoy the abundance of the life God's given us.

Day 21: Pixie Dust

Pray for pixie dust today. Ask God to shower you with his grace, favor, and delight. Then live wide-eyed for the unexpected ways God may answer. Live with an awareness of divine expectation today.

Day 22: Sunset

God's creation invites us to open our eyes to ten thousand wonders. Take twenty minutes to carve out time to watch the sunset and admire God's handiwork. Consider setting an alarm so you don't miss it, and invite a friend. You can check online to find out what time the sun will dip below the horizon where you live. Depending on your location, you may want to travel to a hill or tall building nearby to catch a better view. Observe the sky and the shape of the clouds. Watch how the light shifts and changes ever so slowly. Look for colors and hues, even if it's a cloudy day. Spend a few moments thanking God for his wondrous goodness and gifts—which he shares with all of humanity day in and day out. Upload a photo of the sunset and use the hashtag #livewonderstruck.

Day 23: Generosity

Wonder thrives in the element of surprise. Give a joyful gift to someone who least expects it! Stop by a coffee shop or local restaurant and purchase a few gift cards. They don't have to be large amounts. Then spend some time asking God who you should give them to. Keep an eye out for unsuspecting people all around you and look for the opportunity to be a conduit of God's blessing and goodness.

Day 24: Forgiving Others

Forgiveness unlocks the wonder of God in our lives. Spend twenty minutes asking the Holy Spirit to reveal any people, situations, or organizations in your life where you harbor unforgiveness. On a blank piece of paper, write them down as they come to mind. Write until you can't think of any more, and then forgive each one. Ask God to forgive you for holding unforgiveness in your heart. Then spend some time blessing each one. Don't wait another day to experience the wonder of forgiveness.

Day 25: Meaning

Though we are given names before or shortly after we emerge from the womb, our names are often reflections of who God has created us to be or the work God wants to do in our lives. Do you know the meaning of your name? If not, take a moment to search for the meaning of your name online. Then spend ten minutes prayerfully reflecting on how God has demonstrated his love and goodness in the meaning of your name as well as who he has called and created you to be. Take time to reflect on the wonder of God's plan and provision for you.

Day 26: Kindness

Love is laced with wondrous discoveries of God's handiwork. Consider the people in your life—especially those you don't naturally connect with or who intimidate you. Go out of your way to express kindness to that person today. Demonstrate God's goodness and love in a practical, tangible way. Reflect on how your actions affect your attitude with this person and celebrate the wonder of relationship.

Day 27: Sitting with God

We spend a lot of time with our spouses, coworkers, and children, but we often miss opportunities to simply *be* with God. Go to a place where God is most real to you—church, chapel, at the beach, or in the subway. Take twenty minutes today to sit beside your Maker. Allow prayers, worship, thanksgiving to emanate naturally from your soul. And, of course, don't forget to pray for wonder.

Day 28: Gratitude

Gratitude is the acknowledgment of God's wonder in our lives. It keeps us from walking past wonder unaware. Set an alarm every three hours throughout your day. Whenever the alarm goes off, write down three things you're grateful for today. Such a simple discipline invites the wonder of gratitude to blossom in our lives.

Day 29: Listen

Flip through your music collection and select a song that's particularly meaningful to your spiritual journey. Close your eyes and listen to the lyrics and the tune. Reflect on the phrases or words that catch your attention. Consider how this song reminds you of God's presence and faithfulness in your life. Spend some time thanking God for his faithfulness in your life.

Day 30: Serve a Stranger

Thankfulness beckons us to discover the wonders of God. The wonder of gratitude isn't just found in expressing thanks to God but also to each other. Find a missionary or person in the military that you, a friend, a family member, or your church knows. Write a letter expressing gratitude and encouraging this person serving overseas. Consider asking if there's anything the person needs and sending a care package. You may even want to pray for the person regularly. Live the wonder of gratitude by expressing thanks to a stranger.

Wherever we find God, we should celebrate his presence. We should share our stories and encourage others to awake to the wonders of God all around us. My hope is that through this thirty-day challenge you, too, will pray for wonder and find yourself awestruck by God in more ways than you ever imagined.

Remember to #livewonderstruck.

BEHIND THE SCENES

Contents

1. If you're intrigued by the unusual numbering of the chapter titles, you're not alone. Several readers have asked me, "Why do you call chapter 1 '.001'?" Here's the scoop: I began numbering my chapters this way in 2007 when I wrote *The Organic God*. Other books that feature this detail include *The Sacred Echo*, *Scouting the Divine*, and *Hungry for God*. I chose this numbering system because I liked the clean layout and design, and I wanted to subtly communicate to you, the reader, *Slow down. Pay attention to the details. This isn't like other books you've read. Don't rush—you'll miss the hidden treasures within.* Since then, the books I pour my whole self into all share this style of chapter numbering. These are the books my best friends read and say, "I didn't know that about you." When you see this numbering, know that you're getting the treasures I've dug the deepest to mine in life and faith.

.000: Captured by the Night Sky

1. I discovered that these mysterious night illuminations begin on the surface of the sun when a cloud of gas is emitted. Whenever that cloud reaches the earth and collides with our planet's magnetic field, the energized atoms create mesmerizing colors and patterns. Alaska is famed for its northern lights, and the best time to see them is on a clear night in the winter, when the days are shortest.

2. Philippians 1:6.

.001: Hidden Among the Highlands | the wonder of divine expectation

1. This is Mary Poppins's word *supercalifragilisticexpialidocious* backward.

2. *Sesame Street's* the Amazing Mumford is a purple magician with pronounced black eyebrows whose magic tricks all too often go awry. With his overeager assistant, Grover, at his side, the Amazing Mumford declares, "A la peanut butter sandwiches!" and a puff of smoke appears. When the scene clears, viewers can see how yet another magic trick has gone wrong. Some of

the Amazing Mumford's more celebrated tricks include making four pine-apples disappear one by one so kids can learn subtraction. My favorite is when the Amazing Mumford waves his wand over a glass cookie jar, which becomes full, then empty again, much to the frustration of *Sesame Street* cohort Cookie Monster. This detail might be important for any children who are enjoying the book alongside of you.

    3. Mark 10:1–16.

    4. Mark 10:16.

.002: Shock and Awe | the wonder of God's presence

    1. For me, the phrase "on the throne" reminded me that God was still in charge, God still had things under control, God still held the whole world in his hands.

    2. Exodus 3:2–4.

    3. Exodus 5:22, emphasis added.

    4. Job 1:20–21.

    5. Job 13:25 MSG.

    6. Job 3:11 paraphrased.

    7. Job 13:24 paraphrased.

    8. Job 7:21 paraphrased.

    9. Job 7:19 paraphrased.

    10. Job 24:1–12 MSG paraphrased.

    11. Job 38:4 paraphrased.

    12. Job 38:6 paraphrased.

    13. Job 38:25 paraphrased.

    14. Job 38:37 paraphrased.

    15. Job 38:41 paraphrased.

    16. Job 39:5 paraphrased.

    17. Job 38:12 paraphrased.

    18. Job 38:19 paraphrased.

    19. Job 40:4 paraphrased.

    20. I find great comfort in a single extraordinary sentence of Frederick Buechner concerning Job: "As for the children he had lost when the house blew down, not to mention all his employees, he never got an explanation about them because he never asked for one, and the reason he never asked

for one was that he knew that even if God gave him one that made splendid sense out of all the pain and suffering that had ever been since the world began, it was no longer splendid sense that he needed because with his own eyes he had beheld, and not as a stranger, the one who in the end clothed all things, no matter how small or confused or in pain, with his own splendor." From *Peculiar Treasures: A Biblical Who's Who* (San Francisco: Harper San Francisco, 1979), 77.

21. Thank you for honoring my privacy in such matters. I don't wish to share more about the illness.

.003: Alpenglow Evenings | the wonder of creation

1. Psalm 1:3.
2. Psalm 90:5–6.
3. Psalm 51:2.
4. Marc Berman, John Jonides, and Stephen Kaplan, "The Cognitive Benefits of Interacting with Nature," *Psychological Science* 19, no. 12 (2008): 1207–12.
5. M. Bodin and T. Hartig, "Does the Outdoor Environment Matter for Psychological Restoration Gained Through Running?" *Psychology of Sport and Exercise* 4 (2003): 141–53.
6. Kathryn Rose and Ian Morgan, "Outdoor Activity Reduces the Prevalence of Myopia in Children," *Ophthalmology* 115, no. 8 (2008): 1279–85.
7. Richard Louv, *The Nature Principle: Human Restoration and the End of Nature-Deficit Disorder* (Chapel Hill: Algonquin, 2011), 11.
8. Psalm 36:5.
9. Psalm 33:5.
10. Psalm 36:6.
11. Psalm 103:12.
12. Psalm 74:12–17, 29:3–9.
13. Psalm 148:6–8.
14. Psalm 107:23–30.
15. Psalm 1:4, 32:9.
16. Proverbs 25:14.
17. Proverbs 17:12.
18. Psalm 84:1–4.

19. Matthew 6:26, 10:29.

20. 1 John 1:5.

.004: A Sanctuary in Time | the wonder of rest

1. See, for example, Genesis 1:5, 8, 13.

2. Abraham Joshua Heschel, *The Sabbath* (New York: Farrar, Straus & Giroux, 1951), 14.

3. Here's Leif's almost-world-famous recipe for green chili chicken.

> 4 trimmed chicken breasts (no excess fat)
> 1 diced medium onion
> 1 tsp. red pepper flakes
> 4 tbsp. taco seasoning
> 1 bay leaf
> 4 cups of chicken broth
> 1 27-oz. can of whole green chiles

> Place first six ingredients in slow cooker and cook on high for 4 hours or more. With slotted spoon remove chicken and onion mixture and place in a container. Discard the bay leaf and all cooking liquid. Place entire can of green chiles including liquid into a blender and puree. Pour green chile puree into slow cooker. Add chicken and onions back in. Heat for 20 minutes or until warm. Shred chicken using two forks while in the slow cooker. Serve with heated corn tortillas, lettuce, tomato, avocado, cilantro, and lime (optional).

4. Some may not be able to take a full day off, but perhaps two half-days are possible. Everyone's Sabbath will look different, but the invitation is to set aside time for rest and worship.

.005: Forgotten Longings | the wonder of prayer

1. Stephen H. Shoemaker, *Finding Jesus in His Prayers* (Nashville: Abingdon Press, 2004), 40. I'm incredibly grateful for Shoemaker's book that accompanied me throughout this season in my life, shaping and influencing much of the material in this chapter.

2. One of our friends makes her own handmade candy bars in small batches and pays close attention to the geographic origin and quality of every ingredient. Check out her delicious work at beesandbeans.com.

3. Abraham Heschel, *Man's Quest for God* (New York: Scribner, 1954), 6–7.

4. Psalm 46:10 KJV.

5. Psalm 42:7.

6. John 11:41–42.

7. Mark 14:36.

8. Luke 23:34.

9. Matthew 27:46 NIV.

10. Luke 23:46 NIV.

11. For a more in-depth look at the prayers of Jesus, check out the *Wonderstruck* 7-week DVD curriculum from LifeWay, which invites participants to explore the prayers. You can learn more about and order the curriculum at margaretfeinberg.com.

12. Leon Morris, *Luke: Tyndale New Testament Commentaries* (Downers Grove, Ill.: InterVarsity Press, 1988), 211.

13. Matthew 6:9–13. The version in Luke 11:2–4 is even shorter. Please note that I added the word *Abba* before *Father* to emphasize the intimate relationship Jesus enjoyed with God. The Greek word used is *pater*, which means "father," but in Aramaic, the word is *Abba*, which can be translated "Dad," or almost as "Daddy." Also, the doxology of the Lord's Prayer is, "For Yours is the kingdom and the power and the glory forever. Amen." This mention is not included in the Gospel of Luke or the earliest manuscripts of Matthew but was added later, as noted in Matthew 6:13.

14. Matthew 6:7 NIV.

.006: Treasure Hunting in Africa | the wonder of restoration

1. See Ezekiel 37.

2. Ezekiel 37:3.

3. The Torah forbids the mistreatment of the blind. Giving misleading directions or doing anything to cause a blind person to stumble was strictly prohibited. See Deuteronomy 27:18 and Leviticus 19:14.

4. Kenneth E. Bailey, *Jesus Through Middle Eastern Eyes: Cultural Studies in the Gospels* (Downers Grove, IL: InterVarsity Press, 2008), 172–73.

5. Mark 10:47.

6. Mark 10:51.

7. Mark 10:52 NIV.

8. Mark 10:46, 52.

9. Matthew 10:8.

.007: Magic in the Table | the wonder of friendship

1. John 10:1–7, Revelation 3:20, Luke 13:24.

2. Genesis 4:7.

3. Genesis 7:15–16, Genesis 19:9–10.

4. Revelation 3:14–21.

5. John 15:15.

6. Abraham is called God's servant (Genesis 26:24) and friend (Isaiah 41:8). Prophets were referred to as servants (2 Kings 17:13), and the nation of Israel was collectively referred to as servants (Isaiah 41:8–9), but individuals called the Lord's servant were rare (Moses: Exodus 14:31; David: 2 Samuel 7:5; Isaiah: Isaiah 20:3). In Exodus 33:11, Moses comes close to receiving the title of friend, but it's not a direct address—it's a simile.

7. Matthew 11:28–30.

8. Insights on the yoke are from Michael Blewett, "The Declaration of Inter-Dependence," preached July 3, 2011. Check out Michael Blewett's blog at michaelblewett.com.

.008: The Disappearing Silver Necklace | the wonder of forgiveness

1. Matthew 18:21. In the parable that follows Peter's question (vv. 23–35), some translations use the word *servant*. The NASB is among those translations that use the word *slave*.

2. Mark 11:25.

3. John 20:23.

4. Eugene Davidson is not this man's real name. In considering an alternative, I confess to being tempted to call him "Richard Boils" or some other name that carried a double meaning. But I chose to call him Eugene

because it's reminiscent of the Greek word *Eulogeo*, meaning "blessing," and *David*, meaning "beloved." Luke 6:28 challenges us to bless those who curse us, and in this case, I decided to follow the words of Jesus literally.

.009: Miracle on the Runway | the wonder of gratitude

    1. 1 Thessalonians 5:16–18, emphasis added.

    2. Galatians 5:22.

    3. Gene L. Green, *The Letters to the Thessalonians: The Pillar New Testament Commentary* (Grand Rapids, MI: Eerdmans, 2002), 257–60.

    4. Romans 8:31–39.

    5. Acts 16:9.

    6. Green, *Letters to the Thessalonians*, 12.

    7. A.S. F. Gow, and D. L. Page, eds., *The Greek Anthology: The Garland of Philip and Some Contemporary Epigrams* (Cambridge: Cambridge University Press, 1968), 1:329.

    8. Acts 16:25.

    9. Psalm 13:1–2.

    10. Psalm 13:3–4.

    11. Psalm 13:5–6.

.010: The Legend of Cactus Jack | the wonder of abundant life

    1. Although it doesn't mention my great-grandfather's loan to Publix's founder, its history is told at publix.com.

    2. John 10:10.

SOUNDTRACK

Music awakens the heart. This list of songs suggests music to accompany your journey through the chapters of *Wonderstruck*. If you find a few other songs that are great fits, please let me know at wonderstruck@margaretfeinberg.com.

.000: Captured by the Night Sky

"Take Me Into the Beautiful," Cloverton, *Take Me Into the Beautiful*

"Bring on the Wonder," Sarah McLachlan, *Laws of Illusion*

"Beautiful Things," Gungor, *Beautiful Things*

.001: Hidden Among the Highlands | the wonder of divine expectation

"Raconte-Moi Une Histoire," M83, *Hurry Up We're Dreaming*

"Wonder of the World," Rush of Fools, *Wonder of the World*

"Hallelujah," Rufus Wainwright, *Shrek—Music from the Original Motion Picture*

.002: Shock and Awe | the wonder of God's presence

"Hello Hurricane," Switchfoot, *Hello Hurricane*

"Still," The Fray, *Scars & Stories*

"Show Me What I'm Looking For," Carolina Liar, *Coming to Town*

.003: Alpenglow Evenings | the wonder of creation

"What a Wonderful World," Louis Armstrong, *All Time Greatest Hits*

"Orange Sky," Alexi Murdoch, *Time Without Consequence*

"Stars in the Sky," Kari Jobe, *Where I Find You*

.004: A Sanctuary in Time | the wonder of rest

"Shake it Out," Florence and the Machine, *Ceremonials*

"First Breath After Coma," Explosions in the Sky,
Earth Is Not a Cold, Dead Place

"You Can Have Me," Sidewalk Prophets, *These Simple Truths*

.005: Forgotten Longings | the wonder of prayer

"With Everything," Hillsong, *Aftermath*

"The Prayer," Celine Dion (with Andrea Bocelli), *These Are Special Times*

"Whenever I Say Your Name," Sting (with Mary J. Blige), *Sacred Love*

.006: Treasure Hunting in Africa | the wonder of restoration

"Bronte," Goyte, *Making Mirrors*

"Hello World," by Lady Antebellum, *Need You Now*

"Mercy," OneRepublic, *Dreaming Out Loud*

.007: The Magic in the Table | the wonder of friendship

"Don't Stop Believin'," Journey, *Greatest Hits*

"Boston," Augustana, *All the Stars and Boulevards*

"Decimate," David Ford, *Songs for the Road*

.008: The Disappearing Silver Necklace | the wonder of forgiveness

"Fire to the Rain," Adele, *21*

"The Cave," Mumford and Sons, *Sigh No More*

"Say," John Mayer, *Say*

.009: Miracle on the Runway | the wonder of gratitude

"Paradise," Coldplay, *Mylo Xyloto*

"Wherever You Will Go," The Calling, *Wherever You Will Go*

"'Tis So Sweet to Trust in Jesus," Casting Crowns, *The Altar and the Door*

.010: The Legend of Cactus Jack | the wonder of abundant life

"Closing Time," Semisonic, *Feeling Strangely Fine*

"The Gambler," Fun, *Aim and Ignite*

"Hear You Me," Jimmy Eat World, *Jimmy Eat World*

SPECIAL THANKS

THANKS TO SO MANY who yelled and cheered, shouted and jeered, as these words and images took form. I'm grateful to Troy and Suzanne Champ for their wit, friendship, and library (sorry about scuffing some of those book covers, Troy!). Thanks to Sarah and Roger Johnson, who opened their home so we could explore their city and write, write, write. Thanks to Shelley Fillafet for praying me through every chapter—your prayers are potent. Special thanks to Carol and Marty Rykiel, who continue to make this journey with us. Gratitude abounds toward Jonathan Merritt for helping give birth to this book's format in a kids' Sunday school room. I can't think of a better place to dream up a book on wonder. Your support along the way still makes me well up.

Thanks to Chad Allen, who shared his editing brilliance in the final chapter. Thanks to Tracee Hackel, Abby Reed, Dave Terpstra, Scot McKnight, Byron Borger, Jennifer Grant, Shauna Neiquist, Jimmy Stewart, Kris Bearss, and Craig Blomberg for their careful read-throughs and to Mark Blitch for song suggestions.

Thank you to my friend Michael Blewett, who reminded me that my grandfather wasn't too different from a lot of biblical characters.

Thanks to Jessica Johnson, affectionately known to everyone else as "Our Jessica," who continues to push, pull, and poke at the mysteries of faith all the while holding our office team (and me) together.

Thank you to Angela Scheff, my much adored editor, who has mastered the art of celebrating strengths and saving me from myself—my humble ovation for your every brushstroke.

Gratitude flows toward those I've not yet had the privilege of meeting. To Frederick Buechner—you've arrested me with the greatness of communicating God's love, and as thanks, I promise to never stop sprouting wild and unexpected vines. To Walter Brueggemann—you provide gravel for my soul. When I hear the rumble, I'm reminded of the importance of this long, desolate, dusty journey. To Stephen Shoemaker—if I could wrap my arms around your neck, I don't know that I would ever let go. Your deep, rich voice resonates so deep inside of me. To Nelson Mandela—you've taught me that the script of life is meant to be broken, must be broken, if people are to be set free. To Elie Wiesel—should our paths cross in heaven I think I'd be tempted to hold one of your hands forever. To Abraham Heschel—you awaken a love for God in me like few others.

Thanks to Chris Ferebee, who continues to ride faithfully along in this wild roller coaster known as publishing. Thank you to the team at Worthy, who continues to take big risks; your passion for aesthetics and quality intoxicate me. You all speak my love languages.

Thanks to Marjane, Bill, Coke, and Gary, whose ongoing support means so much. Infinite kisses to my Leif, endearingly known as Leifington, who continues to embark on this grand life with me each day. I love you more than you will ever know. And to Hershey, our superpup, who shows no worldly concern as much writing is accomplished while he's napping nearby.

And thanks to you, my dear readers, who continue the journey of this wondrous life of faith: As I enjoy the privilege of serving you, talking with you, asking of you, your warmth is felt across the scant landscape and distant seas. Your words and notes and blogs and tweets and participation in my Bible studies mean more than you could know.

On this side of heaven, may I shout with the mightiest of roars: thank you.

CONNECTION

Margaret Feinberg is a popular Bible teacher and speaker at churches and leading conferences such as Catalyst, Thrive, and Extraordinary Women. Her books and Bible studies have sold more than six hundred thousand copies and received critical acclaim and extensive national media coverage from CNN, the Associated Press, *USA Today*, the *Los Angeles Times*, the *Washington Post,* and more.

Christianity Today recently listed her among "50 Women to Watch," *Charisma* magazine named her one of the "30 Emerging Voices" who will help lead the church in the next decade, and *Christian Retailing* magazine included her in the "Forty Under Forty" who will shape Christian publishing. Margaret currently lives with her husband, Leif, and their superpup, Hershey, in Morrison, Colorado. She says one of her greatest joys is hearing from readers. So go ahead and drop her a note at:

wonderstruck@margaretfeinberg.com

WORTHY
PUBLISHING

IF THIS BOOK TOUCHED A CHORD IN YOUR LIFE, WILL YOU CONSIDER SHARING THE MESSAGE WITH OTHERS?

- Mention the book in a Facebook post, Twitter update, Pinterest pin, or blog post.

- Recommend this book to those in your small group, church, workplace, and classes. Invite a group of friends to do the Wonderstruck Bible study together.

- Head over to facebook.com/margaretfeinberg, "LIKE" the page, and post a comment as to what you enjoyed the most.

- Tweet "I recommend reading #livewonderstruck by @mafeinberg // @worthypub"

- Pick up a copy for someone you know who would be challenged and encouraged by this message.

- Write a review on amazon.com or bn.com.

You can subscribe to Margaret's newsletter at www.margaretfeinberg.com.

You can subscribe to Worthy Publishing's newsletter at www.worthypublishing.com.

WORTHY PUBLISHING
FACEBOOK PAGE

WORTHY PUBLISHING
WEBSITE

MargaretFeinberg.com

Great Resources for You, Your Book Club, and
Your Small Group at www.margaretfeinberg.com.

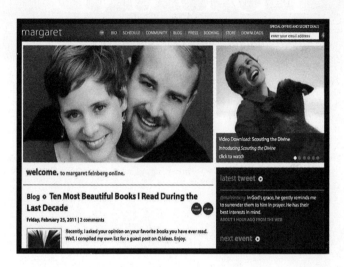

On the site, you'll find:

Margaret's Personal Blog
Speaking Schedule
Weekly Giveaways

E-Newsletter Sign-Up
Video and Audio Clips
Great Prices on Bible Studies

Become a fan on Facebook
facebook.com/margaretfeinberg

Follow on Twitter
@mafeinberg

Follow on Pinterest
pinterest.com/mafeinberg

Follow on Instagram
@mafeinberg

To drop Margaret a line, ask a question, or say "Hello,"
email wonderstruck@margaretfeinberg.com.

MargaretFeinberg.com

Great Resources for You, Your Book Club, and Your Small Group at www.margaretfeinberg.com.

Scouting the Divine is a 6-week interactive DVD Bible study featuring 8-10 minute teaching segments that dive deep into the agrarian world of the Bible. Participants find the Bible coming alive as they learn about scripture through the eyes of a shepherd, a farmer, a beekeeper, and a vintner.

The Sacred Echo: Hearing God's Voice in Every Area of Your Life 6-session DVD Bible study features 15-20 minute segments designed to help participants develop a more vibrant prayer life and recognize the repetitive nature of God's voice in their lives.

The Organic God 6-session DVD Bible study featuring 8-12 minute segments looks at the attributes of God, His generosity, wisdom, bigheartedness, beauty, and more. Encounter God like you've never experienced Him before.

Pursuing God's Love: Stories from the Book of Genesis reminds us of the unflinching love of our Creator. Even when we question God's love, God pursues us. This 6-session DVD Bible study features 15-20 minute segments designed to take participants through the entire book of Genesis.

Pursuing God's Beauty: Stories from the Gospel of John offers portraits of salvation, redemption, and restoration. Filmed in an art studio, this 6-session DVD Bible study features 15-20 minute segments designed to take participants through the entire Gospel of John.

Verbs of God: How God Moves on Our Behalf 4-session DVD Bible study featuring 12-15 minute segments looks at verbs in Scripture to highlight that God is always active and engaged in our lives. Even when we can't see or feel Him, God is constantly on the move and working.

To receive a FREE DVD sampler of Margaret Feinberg's DVD Bible Studies, email your mailing address to **sampler@margaretfeinberg.com**.
We'll get one to you.

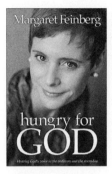
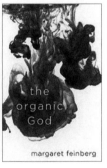